When All Else Fails

When All Else Fails

*Rethinking our Pastoral Vocation
in Times of Stuck*

Wayne L. Menking

WIPF & STOCK · Eugene, Oregon

WHEN ALL ELSE FAILS
Rethinking our Pastoral Vocation in Times of Stuck

Wipf and Stock
An Imprint of Wipf and Stock Publishers
199 W. 8th Ave., Suite 3
Eugene, OR 97401

www.wipfandstock.com

ISBN 13: 978-1-62032-499-8

Manufactured in the U.S.A.

Contents

Foreword

Here is a new paradigm for those engaged in the practices of pastoral care! This book proposes nothing less than a transformative, liberating paradigm shift for all those engaged in the relational work of pastoral care. What Edwin Friedman proposed in relation to a new paradigm for leadership in his book *Failure of Nerve* Wayne Menking accomplishes with keen insight and pastoral wisdom in relation to the field of pastoral care.

In this proposal, pastoral care is a form of work that requires far more than conventional approaches to empathic listening and identification with others. Instead, the key to transforming and liberating pastoral care has everything to do with the recognition that pastoral caregivers have power—not abusive power but healing power—which is only released when they engage others as those who are themselves "empowered agents" rather than "recipients" of their care.

This book builds on the best resources of family systems theory but appropriates the fundamental concepts (emotional systems, anxiety, homeostasis, etc.) and their application to leadership theory (the fallacy of empathy, the fallacy of information, etc.) to develop an original proposal for a new pastoral care paradigm. In this paradigm, the pastoral caregiver adapts less to given circumstances and instead attends in a focused way to the emotional climate. Thereby, "pastoral care is the work of leading people from what is old into what is new, whether they are individuals, families, congregations, or organizations." This bold claim necessitates a shift in perspective from "taking care of" others to genuine "caring for" others, which summons them to take new responsibility for the well being of their own lives. As in the following reference to a particular case, Menking dares pastoral caregivers to take prophetic risks: "In a very paradoxical way, their willingness to confront him with the reality of his life and to thrust him into the pain of recognizing the consequences of his behavior is a profound act of caring." How willing are you, as a pastoral caregiver, to call to accountability those in your care?

Pastoral care in this book involves engaging the principalities and powers of this world that hold others—and ourselves!—in bondage. This means that loving others entails "challenge and confrontation when bad and destructive behavior erupts." Do we care enough about the people with whom we work to name the patterns contributing to their own disease and to their broken relationships with others? This asks much of pastoral caregivers. It requires the honest self-examination of one's own fears about not getting it right or failing. It requires living by trust rather than certainty. It requires abandoning false humility and claiming the power to name clearly the prevailing dynamics, in order to unmask the reality of "stuckness" and challenge others to become authentic selves. This book is nothing less than a wake-up call and summons to personal and professional integrity on the part of those who engage in pastoral care.

Menking is deeply grounded in a compelling theological framework. The God behind this paradigm is not a commodity for sale to the consumers of pastoral care. Instead, here is a God who does not allow "the sufferer to remain stuck in the position of helpless victim." The God of the Beatitudes and the Sermon on the Mount does not heap pity on those who are suffering. Rather, this God hearkens people to become agents by daring to engage already in the resurrected life through turning the other cheek and giving the shirt off their backs, subversive practices that cast off dependencies and invite others to claim freedom as those liberated by God. An integral theology of the cross undergirds this new paradigm, providing solid ground under the feet of those who are prepared to reframe and reclaim their own true selves according to these practices in pastoral care. Without a "transition in the caregiver and leader, change is not likely to happen in the recipient of care. Instead both will likely stay stuck in the chronic condition." Salvation happens when the pastoral caregiver moves beyond "niceness" and shame to relate to other persons as agents, each of whom has been set free by the reality of justification by grace through faith alone. Only through the power of the external Word of God, as enlivened by the power of the Spirit, can all those involved in the pastoral care relationship be transformed and liberated to become the persons God created them to be.

Through clearly written and documented chapters, rich case material, and thought-provoking questions for discussion and reflection, Menking demonstrates how this emerging paradigm of pastoral care, rooted in the authenticity of self on the part of the pastoral caregiver, can lead us from the bondage of dependency relationships through an Exodus into the freedom of life-giving relationships. This approach hearkens the reign of God through the practice of a subversive wisdom in the art of pastoral care. May readers have the eyes to see and the ears to hear!

Craig L. Nessan
Wartburg Theological Seminary
Dubuque, Iowa
Feast of the Resurrection 2013

Preface

This book is for pastoral caregivers and leaders who have found themselves in the condition of stuck. It does not matter whether that stuckness was in working with an individual, a family, a church board or committee, or any other emotional system. It is simply for pastors who in the course of their ministry, in one context or another, have found themselves stuck. By stuck, I mean that condition in which you have found yourself working harder and harder, doing the same old things over and over, and finding yourself reaping the same old results. By stuck, I mean finding yourself in that place where despite your best efforts, nothing changes. The same complainers keep complaining about the same things; the same troublemakers keep making the same trouble; the same victims keep getting victimized by the same things; and all the while you keep working hard and harder to make their complaining, troublemaking, and victimizing go away. If you have found yourself stuck, this conversation may be helpful to you.

It is not written from the position of an expert, but rather from the position of one who has been stuck countless times and one who continues to get stuck. It is written from the position of one who keeps learning and working to stay unstuck. My passion for this conversation is rooted in my own ministry, particularly in those moments where in the interest of peace, harmony, and goodwill, I did not speak with integrity or authenticity. It is rooted in those moments where I did not trust what I was thinking and feeling, particularly in those moments where I did not trust my anger or my dissonant voice that would have raised the anxiety in others. I look back at many of those moments realizing that opportunities for powerful and effective ministry were lost in the interest of niceness. In those moment, the persons entrusted into my care were not well cared for.

I write from the position of one who has heard countless stories of stuck pastors and caregivers. I've heard these stories as the director of the Ministry Development Center of the Southwest, as a CPE supervisor, and as the director of The Lutheran Seminary Program in the Southwest. I also write from the position of one who is concerned about the church and its leadership. From my perspective, we have lost our way. Our mission seems no longer about helping people rise to the occasion so as to withstand the powers that have hold of their life. It seems more and more about helping people feel good, a theme that the reader may well tire of hearing before coming to the end. Yet it simply cannot be said enough: our mission is not about helping people feel good; it is about helping people leave what is old for what is new; it is about helping them find liberation from whatever power threatens to undo their life. And as the reader will soon discover, I do not find the movement from what is old to what is new to come without discomfort, disease, and downright resistance. I speak from experience!

Having heard so many stories of stuckness from pastors and caregivers, I find Friedman's analysis in his book *Failure of Nerve* to be right on track.[1] It was a liberating book for me to read, and as the reader will discover, I speak about and refer to Friedman more from the vantage point of a "disciple" than from the vantage point of a critical thinker. Hopefully this book will reflect critical thinking, but I confess from the outset that this discussion was not undertaken with an eye to critiquing Friedman as much as it was from the position of asking how he can help us rethink our pastoral vocation. To be sure, there are many books and conversations on systems theory that could have been used in developing this discussion. The reader is justified in critiquing me on my narrow selection of resources. However, as I noted, Friedman's works, particularly *Failure of Nerve*, have been liberating for me. They have stimulated me to think theologically in new ways; they have stimulated me to rethink and reframe old doctrinal statements—like justification by grace through faith—in new ways. More than anything, they have challenged me to rethink my pastoral calling and vocation, and it is that challenge that I hope in some way to pass on in this book!

The reader will see that each chapter ends with a series of discussion questions. These are not questions intended to be taken lightly nor are they questions that come with easy and trite answers. They are intended to prompt you into a serious, in-depth, and above all a candid and honest conversation with yourself. I hope that these questions will challenge you to look honestly

1. Throughout this book, all names of persons in all case studies and illustrations have been changed.

at how you came into ministry, what you were expecting, how you have been shaped and formed, and how you have been disillusioned. If you have not done so, I hope they will challenge you into rethinking who you are as a pastor, what your call really is about, and what you need to do to become the authentic pastor God has called you to be! I invite you to tackle these questions with trusted colleagues. Engage these discussions with persons who will not be nice to each other and protect each other, but will engage each other and the conversation with candid honesty.

My hope for you the reader is exactly that: I want to challenge you to rethink your pastoral calling and vocation with candor and honesty, particularly if you find yourself in the condition of stuck. Frankly, I don't like being stuck, and I don't like you being stuck, either. I want freedom and liberation for both of us, and I hope that in some small way this book will contribute to us finding it! More than anything, I want us freed from the shackles and bondages that keep us from speaking truth, and as you will soon discover, the most debilitating shackle I know is the bondage of shame. As with me, I want you freed from that shame so that you can speak your voice without fear of repercussion and consequences! I want us all to rise to the occasion so that we along with those we serve can leave what is old and move into what is new.

Acknowledgments

Over the course of my life, I've had many teachers who have left a lasting imprint, some within the structures of my formal education, others who happened along the way and didn't realize they were teaching. I am grateful to them all. I am especially grateful to Jim Anderson (deceased) and Mark Anderson, two valued CPE supervisors who helped me get unstuck at a particularly difficult time in my life. They knew how to speak truth at the right time.

I am also grateful to two colleagues that I came to know and deeply appreciate during my eight years at the Lutheran Seminary Program in the Southwest: Dr. Kathleen Billman of the Lutheran School of Theology at Chicago and Dr. Craig Nessan of Wartburg Theological Seminary. I came to appreciate their wisdom and support in so many ways. As this book evolved, both provided valued consultation through their suggestions and sometimes penetrating questions. I am honored and grateful that they have written the foreword and the afterword.

Lastly, and most importantly, I am grateful to my family, my wife Nancy, and my four children: Scott, Wendy, Andy, and Lauren. One day, Nancy finally tired of hearing me say, "someday I'm going to write a book," so she said, "write it or shut up." Talk about helping someone get unstuck! Without her encouragement and helping me set time aside to write, this project would not have been possible. Likewise, I am indebted to my children for their encouragement. Each in his or her own way has stretched my thinking and helped me see things through different lenses. We have all had our moments of being stuck, sometimes individually, sometimes together; through it all I have come to admire their tenacity and their courage to speak truth. For all of you, my gratefulness is beyond words.

One

Our Vocation Challenged— Rethinking What We Are About

The Condition of Stuck

In his book *The Failure of Nerve* Ed Friedman noted that ours is a society of quick fixes and easy answers that seek comfort over challenge. Friedman observed:

> The climate of contemporary America has become so chronically anxious that our society has gone into an emotional regression that is toxic to well-defined leadership. This regression, despite the plethora of self-help literature and many well-intentioned human rights movements, is characterized principally by a devaluing and denigration of the well-differentiated self. It has lowered people's pain thresholds, with the result that comfort is valued over the rewards of facing challenge, symptoms come in fads, and cures go in and out of style like clothing fashion.[1]

From Friedman's perspective, this toxic climate is a subtle yet serious threat to the survival of the human species.

1. Friedman, *Failure of Nerve*, 53.

In making such a statement, he is not an over indulging alarmist. Rather, he makes this claim having observed that there is within the very nature of the life process an instinctual immunity that has served to defend the self against anything that would threaten its life and integrity.[2] This immunity is threatened by society's willingness to adapt to the immature desire for quick fixes, easy answers, and the inability to stand amid dis-ease and discomfort. The threat is internal, not external.

This book posits that Friedman's observations and analyses have direct implications for the work of pastoral care and leadership, particularly when ministers find themselves in the condition of stuck. My observation is that pastors who find themselves in this condition—and most of us must confess that we have been in this condition at one time or another—have succumbed to the very things that Friedman identifies: we have adapted to demands for quick fixes, easy answers, and parishioners' inability to stand amid dis-ease, discomfort, and anxiety. As we shall see, this adaptivity has caused us to deter from our pastoral office and vocation.

"Adaptation" and "adaptivity" are terms that will be used throughout this discussion so it is important to define them. Without question, effective leadership calls for adaptation to rapidly changing environments and circumstances. This is what I might call intentional and strategic adaptation. The leader or caregiver intentionally decides to adapt to a set of circumstances, but knows why she is making the adaptation. The adaptation serves a longer-term goal or mission. The adaptivity to which I will

2. Ibid., 182.

refer is not of that sort. It is less a strategic adaptation to circumstances and more of an adaptation to an emotional climate. This kind of adaption generally serves the purpose of restoring an immediate emotional balance to the system by creating consensus and harmony as opposed to serving a long-term goal or objective. It is a resistance to the dis-ease and anxiety that comes with a change in the homeostatic balance of an emotional system. When leaders and caregivers adapt in this way they are generally trying to avoid their own anxiety around the discomforts that are inherent in change.

A vignette from my supervisory practice will illustrate how this adaptivity works and the extent to which its subtleness keeps it almost hidden. A student I was supervising was stuck. As much as she had been made aware of behavior patterns that were adversely affecting her pastoral care, she would not change, choosing instead to remain in old, familiar and comfortable patterns that were unhelpful to her pastoral functioning. In her training process she continued to be challenged by peers and supervisors, at times with intensity. In these moments her almost immediate and knee-jerk response to the confrontations was to say with tears how grateful she was for our investment in her process and how much she appreciated the feedback. I came to realize that these expressions of appreciation and gratitude were actually the means by which she sought to restore her homeostatic balance and avoid the anxiety of the moment. More to the point, she was attempting to win the approval of her peers and supervisors through her gratefulness, but in the process avoided the learning that would lead to necessary changes if she was to move towards her stated goals.

What is more important is the extent to which my adaptivity to her niceness and gratefulness contributed to her resistance to change. In these moments of confrontation and challenge, I adapted to her tears by sympathizing with her, letting her know that I understood her situation, and reassuring her that she was a good student who would eventually get to where she wanted to go. My adaptivity to her feelings helped remove her dis-ease, the very dis-ease that would have facilitated her learning. I went from a position of challenge to a position of rescuer. Between her gratefulness and my sympathetic support, we diminished the anxiety that held the potential for change. Just as she retreated to a familiar position, so did I. We both adapted to the anxiety and dis-ease of the moment by retreating to comfortable and familiar positions.

Thus, the adaptivity to which I will refer throughout this discussion is an adaptivity that retreats from anxiety, seeks to diminish if not remove it altogether, and works to restore the emotional system to its homeostatic balance of security and good feelings. As the vignette illustrates, this kind of adaptivity gives rise to stuckness.

Friedman's observations about the condition of stuck are helpful to our discussion. He notes that ours is an "imaginatively gridlocked" society.[3] Any system that is stuck in such a gridlock will evidence three common characteristics: the system works harder and harder using old ways of thinking and doing; it continues to seek answers through old ways of thinking rather than reframe questions and problems; and it is increasingly polarized

3. Ibid., 33.

by either/or thinking that creates false dichotomies.[4] Observing these characteristics at work at all levels of our society, his thesis is:

> Leadership in America is stuck in the rut of trying harder and harder without obtaining significantly new results. The rut runs deep, affecting all the institutions of our society irrespective of size or purpose. It even affects those institutions that try to tackle the problem: universities, think-tanks, and consultants. These institutions are "stuck" and there exists a connection between the paralysis that leaders experience and the paralysis in the thinking processes of those who would get them unstuck.[5]

Whether in simple emotional systems such as the one that existed between the student and me, or more complex systems such as congregations and religious institutions, or even the broader and significantly more complex system of a nation, there seems to be a growing incapacity to imagine ourselves beyond what we know and with which we are familiar. Our increasing need for comfort and quick fixes inhibits us from imagining anything that would call us forth into new ways of thinking and being. We, therefore, adapt to our resistance and continue to recycle old ways of thinking and being that prevent us from change. In short, we stay stuck.

Many pastors know something about the condition of stuck! We know ourselves to be in this condition when we come to the stark realization that despite our best efforts, the circumstance we have been trying to affect does

4. Ibid.
5. Ibid., 3.

not change. More to the point, we come to the realization that our best efforts are not even able to create in others a desire to change. We know ourselves to be in the condition of stuck when we see old patterns of behavior and chronic conditions continue to recycle themselves despite our best intentions and efforts to change. We know the condition of stuck when in our exasperation we find ourselves screaming internally and externally, "I don't know what else to do!"

This moment of stuckness can come when working with a recalcitrant congregation attempting to resolve a long-standing conflict. The pastor has extended what she sees as all possible options for resolution only to find that there are those who want to perpetuate the conflict for its own sake. They are bent on perpetuating the chronic condition and the pastor is helpless to change that desire. The moment of stuck can come when working with an individual or a family that has sought help. Despite their stated desire and the pastor's best effort, those to whom the pastor is extending his help find the required change to be more painful and challenging than their current condition, so nothing happens. Yet they blame him for their problem since he was not able to offer an easy answer or fix to the situation. The moment of stuck can come as the pastor does all that she knows to do to improve preaching, teaching, or pastoral visitation so as to adapt to complaints about her pastoral functioning. Despite her well-intentioned and noble efforts, the complainers are not satisfied and their chronic complaining continues. The list of circumstances around which pastors have experienced stuckness could go on and on. It seems to come with the turf.

This discussion takes as a starting point one of Friedman's stories called "The Bridge."[6] This is a story of a man who, while discovering his long-sought vocation, finds himself "holding the rope" at the other end of which dangles a man. The man has jumped off a bridge, yet wants to be saved from falling into the river below. The man who has jumped assumes no responsibility to help himself. As the story goes, the man in pursuit of his vocation is in a quandary: continue the pursuit of his life vocation or assume responsibility for the other and hold on to the rope. In the end, the decision to let go of the rope and let the other be responsible for his own life is a "when ell else fails" decision. While this moment of decision is a moment of being stuck, it also holds the rich promise of a new way of thinking and being—and dare we say, *salvation*! The quandary is resolved as the man begins to look at the whole situation *and himself* through a new lens, determining whose responsibility belongs to who.

The point of this story, and what is integral to our discussion, is that the man's change in behavior and position towards the other is prompted first and foremost by an internal shift in how he understood himself in relationship to the other. This internal shift empowers him to change his external position, which is that he no longer assumes responsibility for the other and lets the rope go. Getting unstuck from predicaments and moments where we are holding the rope for others is not a matter of finding new external behaviors and techniques. Like the man in the fable, getting unstuck requires a new way of thinking about ourselves, who we are, and what we

6. Friedman, *Friedman's Fables*, 9–12.

7

are ultimately serving. In pastoral language, we call this rethinking our call and vocation. Only when we rethink our call and vocation—what we are to be about—can we begin to change our positions in the emotional systems that are stuck and seemingly have us bound up.

Stuck on Feelings—Empathy and Sympathy

When pastoral caregivers and leaders focus on and adapt to how others are feeling, they will find themselves stuck. Simply put, when the leader or caregiver's primary focus is on how others are feeling, particularly those whose identity and well-being are fused with others, it is generally the case that stuckness follows. Another way to say this is that when leadership becomes adaptive and attempts to find harmony or to remove dis-ease and anxiety altogether, ineffectiveness will prevail.

Yet, pastoral care by its very nature attends to the feelings of others. We are sensitive to people at the point of their deepest need, their moments of hurt, grief, and pain. We seek to bring a "word from the Lord" that will give comfort, light, and hope through the dark moment. That is our work. At the same time, Friedman's observations about stuckness are an important challenge to the vocation of pastoral care. All too often, caregivers fall into the trap of attending to feelings at the expense of leading the one receiving care through their predicament. Moreover, when pastors become adaptive to the dis-ease and anxiety of those they are seeking to help by providing fixes, answers, and palliative comfort, they tend to lose their perspective of the actual predicament. Their ability to help the receiver of care withstand the powers that have hold of his or her life is thereby significantly diminished.

From my perspective, the adaptivity and proclivity of many pastoral caregivers to focus on feelings has two deep and related roots. The first is in our understanding of what constitutes effective pastoral care and leadership. Somewhere along the way, we have acquired the belief that effective pastoral care is about relieving people of their discomfort and dis-ease, regardless of the level at which we are attending to them. Whether we like to admit it or not, the measurement of our pastoral effectiveness is often based on how "good" we have helped others feel. Our "goodness" as pastors is based on others feeling "good," whether it be the result of our care, our preaching, or our organizational leadership. The second has an even deeper root: shame. As we shall see in this discussion, shame is an unconscious and powerful force that drives us to strive mightily for goodness. It is a shadowy force that is often masked by a desire and "call" to help others feel good. For many pastoral caregivers and leaders, the desire to help others feel good is rooted in the deep and abiding shame they themselves are trying to overcome. It is a simple formula: "I will be good if I can help or make others feel good."

Perhaps one of Friedman's most difficult chapters in *Failure of Nerve* is, "Survival in a Hostile Environment: The Fallacy of Empathy." Taking a rather dim view of empathy, he writes:

> It has generally been my experience that in any community or family discussion, those who are first to introduce concern for empathy feel powerless, and are trying to use the togetherness

> force of a regressed society to get those whom
> they perceive to have power to adapt to them. I
> have consistently found the introduction of the
> subject of "empathy" into family, institutional
> and community meetings to be reflective of,
> as well as an effort to induce, a failure of nerve
> among its leadership.[7]

I am among those who found this chapter problem-
atic. His critique of empathy and those who use it flies
right into the face of pastoral care and pastoral leadership.
Empathic listening is what enables us to hear and understand the circumstance of the other. It is what we are
taught to give and extend. More importantly, we understand our pastoral work to have its roots in God's love and
the way God has dealt with God's people. Throughout all
of Scripture we have a God who is empathic to the needs,
wounds, and scars of God's people, especially when they
are powerless. If pastoral care and leadership are somehow to embody God's love, they cannot do so without
empathy. Having said that, I find Friedman's observations
challenging and helpful to my work as a pastoral leader
and caregiver, especially when I reflect on my own moments of stuckness where my concern for the feelings of
others prevented me from speaking my voice and asserting my leadership. I am in agreement with Friedman that
excessive focus on feelings leads to a failure of nerve. At
the same time, pastoral caregivers and leaders cannot do
away with empathy; it is at the heart of what we do.

In an article published in the *Journal of Mental Health
Counseling*, titled "Empathy and Sympathy: Therapeutic
Distinctions in Counseling," Arthur J. Clark offers help-

7. Friedman, *Failure of Nerve*, 133.

ful contrasts between the two that are relevant to our discussion.[8] Clark notes the contrast between empathy and sympathy in the four dimensions of the counseling process, aim, appraisal, apprehension, and agreement. In each of these dimensions, he observes that empathy tends to facilitate and move the counseling process forward while sympathy tends to protect the client from deeper and more productive therapeutic exploration. So for example, as the counselor works to establish the aim of the counseling process with the counselee, empathy serves the purpose of "expressing understanding of the client" and his circumstance, while sympathy tends to "focus on the client's well-being in difficult or challenging circumstances."[9] While sympathy might be important, it runs the risk of short-circuiting the process if it focuses too heavily on the removal of the immediate discomfort. As the counselor attempts to appraise the nature of the counselee's circumstance, empathy is an "attunement," with the client's feelings and meanings, while "sympathy is a reaction to a client's distress that becomes manifest in mild to intense expressions of feelings of sorrow for the plight of an individual," which will tend to close the door on the therapeutic process.[10] As the counseling process progresses, Clark observes that empathy holds potential for apprehending the client's experience at a deeper level than does sympathy. By contrast, the counselor can be sympathetic without having a full grasp of the counselee's predicament or circumstance. Moreover sympathy runs the risk of being a "superficial and perfunctory expression

8. Clark, "Empathy and Sympathy," 95–97.
9. Ibid.
10. Ibid.

which the counselee can perceive as shallow and trite."[11] Similarly, empathy enables the counselor to understand the counselee's perception of his predicament without necessarily agreeing with it. Sympathy, by contrast, holds the potential for expressing commiseration and agreement with the counselee's perceptions, a dynamic that runs the risk of blocking important therapeutic explorations.[12]

If we think in terms of the contrast between empathy and sympathy, we begin to see that what Friedman was alluding to might actually be sympathy rather than empathy. If we use the language of sympathy and sympathetic protection, it is easy to see that he was right. Those who are unable to take responsibility for their emotional selves will work to get the system to sympathetically protect them from any dis-ease or discomfort that change might bring. Thus, change is sabotaged not only by those who want the protection, but also by those who offer it. The point we shall make in this discussion is that the employment of empathy and even sympathy are necessary for pastoral caregivers and leaders; however, when either the work of *feeling with* (empathy) or *feeling for* (sympathy) becomes sympathetic protection, the very change that the caregiver or leader is trying to affect will be sabotaged and the caregiver or leader will have been a complicit participant in that sabotage.

Another perspective helps view this contrast from a much less clinical perspective, yet with a view towards the place of empathy and sympathy in effecting social change. Motivated by the question of whether or not teaching em-

11. Ibid.
12. Ibid.

pathy can lead to social change, the president of Capital University, Denvy Bowman, initiated what he called the "Empathy Experiment."[13] The experiment was prompted by Bowman's own realization that not enough was being done to help potential leaders prepare for their future in innovative and creative ways, particularly as they face the challenges now upon us, especially the plight of the working poor. Six students were selected for the program and they were partnered with five prominent social agencies in Central Ohio. In and through various intense immersion experiences, the students experienced the realities of those whose lives have been upended by unemployment, poverty, and physical challenge. For example, one student was "kicked out" of her college resident hall for twenty-four hours without resources or help in figuring out how to navigate the predicament. Another was challenged to find three community healthcare agencies without the help of Internet, telephone, or other resources that most of us would take for granted. To be sure, this experiment is being reported in an alumnae magazine that is hardly a critical examination of its process or outcomes. At the same time, what the students reported of their experience and how it impacted them is important to our conversation. The students' most important recognition was how critical empathy is to the process of change. Empathic understanding is what enabled them to move from judgment to engagement. As one student commented, "I never thought about how people need help every day with everyday situations."[14] What appears to have happened in this experiment is that a whole new understanding of the

13. "Can Teaching Empathy Lead to Social Change," 4–8.
14. Ibid.

plight of the working poor was awakened in the students, and this awakening is motivating them to action, even if that action is not yet defined. Perhaps most telling was this observation of the students who participated: "no longer content to sympathize with the working poor, the students were all moved to act in some way on behalf of the working poor."[15] In this statement, the contrast between sympathy and empathy could not be clearer. Empathy opened up an understanding that is leading to action and engagement with the other; sympathy tends to be a pity for the other but tends not to motivate one into action on the other's behalf.

One of the ways we can illustrate the contrast between empathy and sympathy is through the story of the exodus and God's deliverance of the people from Egypt. We know the story. At the very beginning, we read that God heard the cries of the people, and he *knew* their condition.[16] He does not know *about* this condition from a distance. Like the students in the Empathy Experiment, God is awakened to the condition of the people in slavery. He knows of their condition within his own being. Their groaning becomes his groaning; their yearning for freedom becomes his. What God experiences within God's self leads to action. God does not sit still and feel sorry for the people in their condition. God is moved in such a way that God's power is stirred to intervene and lead them from slavery into freedom, from what is old into what is new. I suggest that what we see of God in this part of the story is empathy. God hears, understands, and knows deep within God's self what the people are going

15. Ibid.
16. Exodus 2:25 (RSV).

through and what powers hold them in their grasp. God knows and understands their life circumstance.

We know how the story continues. Leaving what is old for what is new does not come easy. The first test comes when the Egyptians regret their decision and come after the people to return them to their condition of slavery. The emotions of the people quickly change from happiness to fear. God intervenes and they are saved. It would seem that this miraculous intervention would be enough to convince the people that they were in good hands for the duration of the journey. Not so. It does not take long for complaining and whining to emerge. Life is difficult. There is a shortage of food and water and the people seem to believe that a return to their prior condition would be better than what they are now in and the new condition to which God is leading them. At this point in the story, God must contend with a new power and it is not external. It is internal: the inability of the people to withstand the difficulties they are up against, which is manifested in their whining, complaining, and desire to return to homeostatic security. It is precisely at this point in the story that God remains *empathic* to the original condition of slavery and desire for freedom that led to God's intervention; however, God does not become *sympathetic* to their complaining or the fact that the journey is difficult.

If God had extended sympathetic protection, we might imagine a conversation like this:

> *The people*: God, this really has become a much more difficult journey than we expected. We didn't anticipate that things would be so hard. After all, no water or food. We were much better off in Egypt than we are here. Let's just go back. Even as bad as it was, it's not as bad as this.

> *God*: I really am sorry. I understand your pre-
> dicament. It has been hard. The desert is a dif-
> ficult place to be, and I did not mean to make
> life that difficult for you. If you think it will really
> be better for you, I'm okay if you want to return.
> How can I help you?

This is exaggerated and over simplified to be sure, but it makes the point. If God had become sympathetic to the complaints and whining of the people, God would have acquiesced and adapted to their perception that they were not up to the challenge. Without question, their anxiety was real and appropriate. Like in most emotional systems whose anxiety level is raised, the people are not able to directly or non-anxiously communicate this to God. Instead, they allow their fear and anxiety to esca-late and it results in increased complaints and demands. If God had become sympathetic God would have given in to these forces and powers that were trying to return things to homeostatic security.

In suggesting that empathy leads to a failure of nerve on the part of leaders or caregiver, Friedman seems to be talking more about what I am calling sympathetic pro-tection. However, as we have seen, empathy is necessary for effective pastoral care and leadership. Furthermore, empathy does not have to deter leadership or care from helping people move from what is old to what is new, as the story of the exodus so clearly illustrates. Sympathy, on the other hand, runs the risk of sabotage. When care-givers and leaders extend sympathy rather than empathy, they run the risk of giving in to the powers that maintain chronic conditions.

A key driver of sympathetic protection is the need to keep everyone in the emotional system content, happy, and together, a dynamic Friedman refers to as the "forces of togetherness."[17] In any emotional system it is generally the persons who are least self-defined and unable to tolerate the anxiety of chaos and change who will play this card. For many pastors and caregivers, "togetherness" trumps everything. Thus, while they know that change is necessary and that they must say or take certain actions, they refuse to take these risks for the sake of keeping order and peace in the organization. It is no different in families who are facing change. In order to maintain peace, tranquility, and happiness, difficult and anxiety-provoking conversations are driven underground by the sympathetic protection of those who cannot or are completely unwilling to tolerate discomfort. When leadership and caregivers succumb to these forces and the resulting sympathetic protection, they in effect defer their power to those in the system who are least self-defined and least able to tolerate the dis-ease of change.

Let us return for a moment to the exodus story and imagine a conversation that God might have had with God's self while Moses was on the mountain and the people have asked Aaron to build them a new god:

> *God* [upon seeing the rebellion]: Oh my, there is dissension among the people. They really are unhappy and I'm the one who brought it on, what with delivering them out of Egypt and all. I'm concerned about how they feel, and I really don't want their life to be miserable this way. I'm more concerned that they are splitting ranks

17. Friedman, *Failure of Nerve*, 67.

> and turning to another god. Perhaps I need to
> rethink what I'm doing here so that we can all
> stay together as one family.

Again, exaggerated to be sure. But what if God's concern in the story had been keeping everybody one big happy family? What if God had made unanimous good feelings a priority over getting out of Egypt and to the promised land? What if God had made ease and comfort a priority? If this had been the case, the people would never have had to rise to the challenge of getting from what is old to what is new and they would have remained stuck in their chronic condition.

The point I'm making is that *sympathetic protection* and the *forces of togetherness* are closely aligned. If God's priority had shifted from getting the people out of Egypt into the promised land to making sure that everyone was happy and no one alienated, his empathy would have become sympathy. Similarly, when pastoral caregivers and leaders shift their focus from helping people transition from the old into the new to making sure everyone is happy and together, their empathic concern turns to sympathetic protection.

An Illustration—Jan's Story

Jan was a resident in our CPE program. She came to her year of training, as most persons do, with a deep desire to offer care, compassion, and comfort to those grieving, sick, and marginalized. Her desire to offer herself in ministry was rooted in her belief that ministry and pastoral care is to embody the love of Christ to those with whom she is engaged. Her desire is for others to feel loved and accepted by God, regardless of their life circumstance. In short, she wants the recipients of her care to "feel good."

In her practice, such embodiment meant offering unconditional understanding to those whom she encountered, assuring them that whatever the circumstance of their life, God loves and cares for them. Within this model and practice of care, Jan sought to offer unconditional acceptance that did not critique or judge the behavior or situation of the other, believing that such critique and judgment would be a denial of the other's intrinsic self-worth. It was difficult for Jan to set boundaries so as to establish a clear differentiation between herself and others. This often resulted in her carrying excessive emotional burdens.

During her residency Jan experienced a situation in which this model and practice of pastoral care was tested. As in other instances, she encountered an individual who was unwilling to take responsibility for her life situation and emotional self. This person incessantly called Jan for help, to which she unquestioningly responded. As these calls continued and as she dutifully responded, Jan began to pay attention to her feelings and behavior. She found herself increasingly angry at this individual's unwillingness to help herself, and she also recognized her passive disengagement from offering help. To her credit, Jan recognized that not only was the person she was trying to help stuck; she was also stuck. Her attempts to help this individual with care, compassion, and unconditional understanding were coming up empty, and more significantly she began to realize that the harder she worked, the more stuck she became.

As Jan uncovered the layers of this story, she realized the extent to which her own behavior was contributing to the dilemma. Her reluctance to render a word of judgment or to set boundaries that would have challenged the other to take more responsibility was only perpetuating the other's excessive dependency. She became aware of how her unconditional understanding and acceptance were actually forms of sympathetic protection!

But Jan made yet another discovery that was critical for her shift in her pastoral position. Not only was she trapped by the manipulative behavior of the one she was trying to help and her own sympathetic caregiving, she was also trapped by her own belief of what it means to be a pastor whose vocation is to embody the love of Jesus. As she discovered, she uncritically believed that to be a pastor in the name of Jesus meant taking on responsibility for the emotional well-being of others, literally carrying their burdens. Sharing the love of Christ did not include turning emotional responsibility back to those to whom it belongs. Even more specifically, she began to realize the extent to which her theological understanding of the role of a pastoral caregiver did not include or give adequate place for making judgments on inappropriate behavior, or setting clear boundaries between herself and those for whom she cared. Powerfully, Jan began to realize the victimization she felt was not because of the behavior of others; it was because of her own belief about what it means to be an ordained pastor and pastoral caregiver. In the face of the powers she encountered in this individual, she realized change would not come from offering more love, sympathy, or care in the same way old way; change could come only if she began to reframe and rethink for herself what it means to be a pastor and what it means to offer care. This meant rethinking her vocational calling at very deep and basic levels.

I use this story because Jan found herself in the moment of stuck, that same moment in which most of us in ministry find ourselves at one point or another. It is that moment where we come up against forces and powers against which our sympathy, care, understanding and unconditional love are unable to withstand, resist, or otherwise change. Like Jan, the harder we work using old understandings and frameworks, the more trapped, tired, and victimized we become. Like Jan, though, we are not victimized by the behavior and actions of others. We are victimized by our own thinking and theology of our pastoral role.

On the surface this may seem to be the story of a novice in ministry, a young seminarian and CPE student who will eventually grow up, mature, and learn. My observation is that Jan's story is not limited to novitiates. Hers is a story replicated time and time again in the lives and practices of ministers of all ages with all sorts of experiences. To be sure, the circumstances are varied and different, but many in ministry have the same images of pastor and pastoral care as Jan: our "call" is to help others "feel good" about themselves regardless of their condition or circumstance. Alongside this image is the belief that unconditional and uncritical caring will eventually prevail and change things. Like Jan, though, ministers across all spectrums and ages know the angst that comes when, despite these noble efforts, they are unable to affect change.

The powers against which we find ourselves are not limited to individual behaviors in the patients and people we visit. They are present in conflicted and divided congregations, present in groups and individuals who are not happy unless community life is disrupted, present in public discourse among those who sow the seeds of hate and anger, present among those who prey on the sensibilities of others, present in families where the behavior of one destroys life for everyone, present in our national and economic life where the greed of a few destroys life for the whole. The list could go on. It matters not where or in what context: ministers and pastoral caregivers will always find themselves standing in the presence of powers that require resistance. Like Jan, because such resistance is not equated with our images of what it means to be a pastoral caregiver or leader, we become adaptive and eventually find ourselves stuck.

My hope for this discussion is that we can be learners like Jan, recognizing that the condition of stuck and its cause is not "out there" in others, but rather within us. The change we are trying to affect, whether in individuals or congregations, begins when we redefine our vocation and pastoral voice.

The Office and Vocation of Pastoral Care

The vocation of pastoral care, its "office" if you will, is to care for others in the moment of their need. Caregivers seek to embody and extend God's love to those who suffer hurt, pain, dis-ease or any other malady that disrupts life. More specifically, pastoral caregivers seek to strengthen and empower the faith of the hurting and disrupted in order that they may be sustained through their circumstance, and ultimately prevail against the powers that seek to wrest their life away. Extending care is what pastoral caregivers and leaders do. The illustrations offered in this chapter, however, have shown how easy it is, in the name of caring for another, to slip into an adaptivity that maintains the status quo. We have seen how easy it is, in the name of caring for another, to move from empathy to a sympathetic protection that sabotages change. The struggle, therefore, is to live out our vocation and office in such a way that enables us to offer authentic care with integrity, a care that does not succumb to adaptivity or sympathetic protection.

I suggest we begin to think of pastoral care in a way that moves it out of the realm of palliative comfort into a realm where care and leadership are merged. To care is to lead and to lead is to care. From my perspective, pastoral care is the work of leading people from what is old into what is new, whether they be individuals, families, congregations, or organizations. As we shall see in the next two chapters, the idea of leading people from what is old into what is new is consistent with the biblical stories that depict transitions from slavery to freedom, dark to light, and death to life.

Hopefully by now, the reader has recognized that my agenda in this discussion is to help us reframe our understanding of care so that we are enabled to care and lead with authenticity and integrity, that we are able to withstand the powers that be when those powers are threatening the lives of those to whom we are extending our care. In this regard, I want to make an important distinction that will help us gain clarity about the vocation of our pastoral office. I want to distinguish between *caring for* and *taking care of*. At first glance, such a distinction might seem insignificant. Hopefully, the reader will understand its importance after further exploration.

An illustration of the difference between *caring for* and *taking care of* is the intervention that family members often initiate when their loved one is threatened by addiction and addictive behavior. Those who have participated in interventions, either as one being intervened upon or as one intervening, know that they are painful and conflicted occurrences. Those intervening confront the one being intervened upon with very painful realities of his life, realities of which his addiction has caused him to be in utter denial. If the intervention is successful, the one being intervened upon begins to recognize the consequences of his behavior and is thrust into a period of remorse, guilt, and even shame, from which he cannot be protected or rescued. It is being thrust into the pain of these realities that motivates the beginning of therapy and treatment. It is facing the reality that his addiction has caused enormous pain in others that prompts him to seek help. Herein lies the crux of the matter: the success of the intervention depends upon those intervening not to cave in and rescue him from these feelings. To do so is to take care of him and not to care for him. In a very paradoxical way, their willingness to confront him with the reality of his life and to thrust him into the pain of recognizing the consequences of his behavior is a profound act of caring! It is the beginning of new life, yet in the moment he will not be able to recognize it as such. As a matter of fact, it is often the case that the interveners will need to muster strength and courage to withstand the defensive reactions and assaults of the one being intervened upon, and the strength and the courage to stand with him in the disorientation and chaos that will follow.

Thus a very important characteristic of *caring for* that is quite distinct from *taking care of* is that the caregiver does not protect or rescue the one being cared for from the realities of his circumstance. When families intervene upon a loved one, they are intentionally moving towards him, even if that "moving towards" is confrontational and brings intense emotional push back. They move towards their loved one precisely out of their care for him. Caring for another means staying intentionally connected with him even in the most anxious of circumstances. *Taking care of*, on the other hand, is an act of emotional distance. It does not seek to engage difficult realities, but rather seeks to avoid them. Rescue and sympathetic protection, while having the veneer of care and love for the other, actually stay away from the painful realities, thus preventing any possibility of change—and again, dare we say, *salvation!*

The interesting paradox is that *caring for* another will often not look or feel like care at all. For the one being intervened upon, those doing the intervening will initially appear mean, evil, and uncaring. To use systems language, those doing the intervening have decided to break the chronic condition and cycle of fusion. They have decided to move from the position of *sympathetically taking care of* to *authentically caring for*, and with such a change in position the one being intervened upon will do everything he can to get them to return to the homeostatic position. To care for another, as in the case of an intervention, means that the one *caring for* must differentiate herself from the anxieties and pain of the one being cared for. If the caregiver assumes responsibility to protect the one being cared for from these emotions, fusion will result. *Caring for* will become *taking care of,* empathy will turn into sympathetic protection, and the chronic condition of stuckness will prevail.

Simply put, the vocation and office of pastoral care is to *care for* others whether they be individuals, families, congregations, or organizations. The vocation and the office is not to *take care of* them. As we have noted throughout this chapter, when pastors find themselves stuck, their work is not to learn a new technique or offer a new program. Their work is to look inside and critically examine their pastoral vocation and the theology that informs it. Getting unstuck requires an internal shift in how one understands one's self and what one is called to do. In this regard, we as pastors will do well to allow ourselves to be informed by the stories of Scripture. We may find ourselves surprised to discover that the God attested to by these sacred stories is a God of deep and abiding compassion, a God who is empathic towards the human condition and fiercely determined to save life from any power that would wrest it away. Yet they also attest to a God who does not take care of, nor does this God show much sympathy. To an examination of some of these important stories we now turn in the next chapter.

Questions for Discussion and Reflection

1. Think of a time in your pastoral care and leadership when you and the emotional system you were working in have been stuck. This could be with an individual, a family, a leadership group, or an entire congregation. What were the circumstances that led to the stuckness? How did you know you were stuck? What was your position[18] in the system? How did that position contribute to the stuckness?

2. What are your thoughts about *empathy* and *sympathy*? Do you tend to be more empathic or sympathetic in your ministry? Can you think of a time when you *sympathetically protected* an individual or an emotional system from the truth? What happened? Was empathy or sympathy employed in the circumstance you identified above? To what extent did it contribute or not contribute to the stuckness?

3. If truth be told, what might be your prevailing assumption about the office and vocation of pastoral care? How do you see and understand this assumption manifested in your ministry practice? Do you *care for* or do you *take care of*?

4. Have you ever allowed yourself to rethink your pastoral vocation and the assumptions that underlie it? Another

---

18. The notion of "position" in an emotional system does not refer to one's title or job description, or even to one's birth position. It refers to one's role in the emotional system. For example, is one's position that of caretaker, peacekeeper, jester, agitator, etc. Important to the consideration of position is the effect this position has on the rest of the emotional system and its ability to change.

way to put it: have you ever allowed yourself to rethink what you are ultimately serving in your ministry? If so, what precipitated the rethinking? What was it like to rethink your vocational call? What was the outcome of the rethinking?

Two

God Cares Deeply—But You Won't Find Much Sympathy

The Commodified God

In 2001 right after 9/11, I was having a conversation with a gentleman at church, and we were discussing the events that had happened. I made the statement that I thought one of the good things that could come out of the event (if anything good could come out of it!) was that for the first time since WWII, we had the opportunity to understand and experience a reality that most of the world lives with on a daily basis, namely vulnerability to the reality of evil. I went on to suggest that one of the stark realities with which we were being confronted was that the security and well-being that we have long taken for granted was no longer an entitlement. We are no more entitled to immunity from the perils of life than any other human creature. The person with whom I was conversing took offense at my comment and retorted: "We are entitled to it because we can afford it!" I was taken aback by the unashamed candor with which he made his claim.

Yet in hindsight I should not have been so surprised. Such entitlement is embedded into our culture and it is part of the American Dream: we can have anything if we work hard enough for it, regardless of the condition of the rest of the world.

While the immediate context of that conversation was the aftermath of 9/11, this individual's comment speaks to a much deeper belief that has made its way into our thinking and being. The belief is that we are entitled to a life that transcends the realities and perils of human existence including the consequences of our own actions. This is, after all, part and parcel of the pursuit of life, liberty, and happiness. What lies even deeper is the belief that the function of God is to assist us in achieving this ideal. We are entitled to feel good; therefore, God's role and function is to provide us the good feelings to which we are entitled.

In an article written in 1977, Timothy Luke coined "commodified God."[1] He noted that the success of the televangelism movement was—and we might say that it still is—due to its remarkable ability to use the marketing medium of television. He further observed that within this movement, the gospel message is packaged and represented as "healing bodies, mending lives, and changing attitudes," not unlike commercials that sell cars, clothing, and soft drinks.[2] Thus, when our "needs" as we see them are met, we feel cared for. Another way that we can frame this is that whenever we enter into times of dis-ease, challenge, confrontation, pain, or suffering, we expect this

1. Luke, "From Fundamentalism to Televangelism," 206.
2. Ibid.

commodified God to offer sympathetic protection and return us to the homeostatic condition of stability.

As we saw in the last chapter, many pastoral care-givers and leaders function out of the belief that effective pastoral care is about relieving people of their anxiety and dis-ease. Thus, wittingly or unwittingly, whenever the focus of our pastoral care is to help others "feel good," we become brokers and agents for the commodified God of which Luke speaks. As we have already seen, pastoral care that is offered from this position does not generally facilitate change, as we are led to think. Instead it contributes to the perpetuation of the chronic condition. In a consumerist society, commodities that are used to remedy dis-ease and bring well-being do not require any action on the part of the user. The commodity, whatever it is, does all the work, and that is precisely the attraction. Commodities supposedly bring about immediate relief to the situation, but no fundamental or life-altering change on the part of the user is required. So it is with the commodified God: this God is called upon to remedy whatever predicament I might have without any consideration as to what God's action or intervention will require of me. This is precisely the question that the pastoral care brokers of the commodified God fail to put forth as well. By not asking this question, the condition of stuck is allowed to continue even though immediate relief might be found.

God's Love and Care Manifested in Power

The inescapable fact to which the entire biblical story gives testimony is that God is a God of compassion who is deeply moved by the suffering of those whom God has created. In Exodus, we read that God heard the suffering cries of slaves in Egypt and "he took notice of them."[3] This is not a "passer-by" observation. God taking notice means that God is moved to action. God intervenes and takes on the powers that hold Israel in their grasp. Freedom does not come without conflict. When freedom is finally achieved, the journey to the promised land is not easy. On more than one occasion, the Israelites complain about the conditions of their journey, voice their impatience, and even seek out other gods. As we noted in the last chapter, God must not only contend with the powers that held Israel in captivity, he must also contend with Israel's internal powers that seek homeostatic security and relief from the anxiety, dis-ease, and challenge of the journey. I suggest that the internal powers that caused Israel to complain and rebel against God when they faced the challenges of freedom and transition into new life are the very same powers at work within us whenever we are faced with any change, and transition from what is old into what is new. In this regard, pastoral caregivers and leaders stand in the tradition of Moses: we are representatives of this tenacious Holy One who seeks nothing more than freedom for those whom he has created from whatever power threatens their life. Like Moses, our work is to help those who are entrusted to our care to withstand

3. Exodus 2:25 (RSV).

these powers so that they can journey into the new life to which they are being called.

The theme of God's deep and abiding compassion for those who suffer is repeated time and time again throughout Scripture. At the same time, the biblical stories are also clear: the compassion that is felt and extended to those who suffer is not the sort that allows the sufferer to remain stuck in the position of helpless victim. While it is a compassion that feels pity, it is not the sort of pity that perpetuates a victimized attitude on the part of the sufferer. When God's compassion is stirred, more than emotion is stirred: God's power is activated! We might even say that when God's compassion is stirred, God's anger is equally stirred and God moves. To be sure, there are references, particularly in the Psalms that wonder why it sometimes takes God so long to be stirred. Nevertheless, when God's passion is tapped, God does something, and God seems to expect that the one or ones who are being helped will join in the work that it will take to liberate them from whatever it is that has been the source of their struggle.

When God's compassion is stirred and God is compelled to act, it is always the case that God calls forth a new creation and a new reality. The recipient of God's compassion is not pitied, but is given a new reality in which to move and have being. When God hears Israel's cry from the depths of Egypt, God's deliverance involves and requires Israel to live into a completely new reality. Israel is called forth to leave behind something that is old and oppressive and to live into something that is new and free. Not only are they called forth from an old way of life, but they themselves are being transformed. They are no longer slaves and captives. They are free and with that freedom comes the challenge to think of themselves as people with new power, a power that will withstand even the military might of Egypt. Such transformational thinking, as we know, does not come without resistance. The calling forth from what is old and the movement into what is new does not come easily. There is resistance, both on the part of the power that has long held Israel captive, and there is resistance within Israel itself. As already noted, we know the many times they complain and wish to return to the "security" of their old way of life and thinking.

The compassionate God of religious narcissism is seen as a sympathetic God who "feels sorry for us," rather than one who is moved to liberating action. Even more to the point, the sympathetic God is seen as one who accepts us for who we are and who wraps his parental arms around us as if to say, "everything will be ok!" These images are void of the God who is deeply moved to engage the powers that have us in their grasp, and they are equally void of the God who is calling forth and leading us into new creation and reality. Another way to say this is that our contemporary images of God's comfort and support that communicate everything will be okay serve to keep us stuck in the status quo. They do not challenge us to envision the new creations and realities that God is calling forth, whether in our individual lives, our family life, our church life, or our socio-political life. So long as we are told, believe, and adapt to the idea that everything will be okay, not much will change.

The entire biblical narrative gives testimony to a God whose deep and abiding care is manifested in God's calling forth new reality. When God cares, God calls the sufferer forth from what is old into what is new, from old ways of thinking and behaving into new. God's challenges the one being called to think in new ways, to see herself through a new set of lens. For the New Testament, resurrection is the power to live in a new way of life that is contrary to and even subversive to the power structures of the Empire. Those who heard and believed the news of resurrection were transformed in spirit, but that transformation was not disconnected from their physical existence. So for example, those who existed at the bottom of the Empire's political-socio-economic pyramid, those who in the eyes of society and the culture were literally persona non grata, received the news of resurrection and new life with a completely new view of reality. The reality of resurrection called them forth from the shame of their old existence into the dignity and respect of being a citizen of the kingdom of God. Within this new reality, the social order of the empire was inverted and they had their place. The last shall be first and the first shall be last!

The point is that God's care results in something being called forth from what is old into what is new. But we should never discount the fact that leaving what is old and venturing into what is new is dangerous and risky business. Living in the new realities created by resurrection was risky business for the early church. As a matter of fact, those who professed the Way of Jesus put their life on the line. It was as dangerous for them as it was for the people of Israel to leave Egypt and move towards the new reality that God was creating. The powers that be— whether those powers are external or internal—never give up their claim and hold on life without fierce, powerful, and even life threatening resistance. In the face of this resistance, those being called forth often find it easy to cower in fear and return to their homeostatic security. While it is easy to understand and sympathize with this sort of anxious fear, it is astounding to note that God does not have such sympathy.

As the following biblical stories illustrate, God is a God who cares deeply; but the Holy One does not seem to have much sympathy for those who want to stay stuck and held hostage by their own fear. God's care motivates God to act, intervene, and call forth something new from what is old. While God may be well aware of the risks and challenges that will be faced as one makes this transformative journey, God does not extend sympathetic protection to those who want to stay stuck.

Five Biblical Stories

The Beatitudes

Regardless of the version you read, the Beatitudes have had a wide variety of interpretations that generally lead in the same direction: those who live in conditions of poverty, grief, hunger, persecution are to find comfort because they have found favor with God. Some have gone so far as to interpret "blessed" as "happy" so that those who are in these conditions should feel good about it. While it is true that God favors the poor, this sort of interpretation offers palliative comfort without offering hope for change. More to the point: the message is conveyed that those who live in these conditions should passively accept them, knowing they will find something better in the life to come.

Interpretations of the Beatitudes that lean towards this sort of palliative comfort are correct in so far as they identify God's favor for those who are on the margins. They are incorrect, however, to suggest that a person should be content and passively accept their plight in life.

So what does it mean to have found God's favor and blessing? Does it really mean that one should be content with one's station in life, even if that station is one of persecution or hunger? As a Palestinian, Father Elias Chacour has wrestled with this very issue in the context of the Israeli/Palestinian conflict. Growing up, he watched his own father and the town elders passively accept Israeli rule and their displacement of Palestinian families, a passivity he could not accept or live out in his own life, given his understanding of the prophets call for justice and righteousness. Describing his struggle as a Christian, he writes: "I could not join with the violent bands who were now attacking the country, even though I could feel their frustration. But neither could I live by the passive ways of Father and the other elders."[4] Reflecting on the Beatitudes, he finds an answer.

Standing on the Mount of Beatitudes, Chacour imagines the scene as Jesus utters these words. As he is drawn to them, he comes to a realization that changes the direction of his own life: "The Beatitudes were prophecies. Not mere platitudes!"[5] They are prophecies that declare a new reality, turning the tables and restoring human dignity to persons from whom that dignity has been taken away. The "poor in spirit," those who will inherit the

4. Chacour, *Blood Brothers*, 150.
5. Ibid., 151.

coming kingdom, stand opposite of the proud, those who have no need of God. The "meek" are not passive bystanders; they are the ones who, like Moses, engage the powers that be, yet they know that their power is not their own: it is from God.[6] As his reflection continues he is awakened to what he sees as the heart of the Beatitudes: at every turn they are about the restoration of human dignity. "If I were really committing my life to carry God's message to my people, I would have to lift up, as Jesus had, the men and women who had been degraded and beaten down."[7] There it is: in the spirit of the Beatitudes, to be blessed is not to be passively resigned to one's plight in hopes of something in the hereafter; it is to be lifted up into a new reality, now and in the moment. When interpreted in this way, the Beatitudes are words of power and empowerment that call forth new reality, not words of palliative sympathy. They are words that empower the one enslaved by the particular condition to define himself in a new way, and live in a new reality.

I recall preaching a sermon on the Beatitudes through this interpretation, in which I invited the congregation to hear these words through a new lens. More importantly I invited the hearers to imagine what these words of empowerment might mean for their own lives. I began to restate the Beatitudes using contemporary conditions in which persons might find themselves stuck. Since I was a guest preacher, I did not know the particulars of anyone in the congregation, but I made reference to the condition of physical abuse by saying something

6. Ibid.
7. Ibid., 154.

like, "Rise up, you who have been abused and beaten." After the service, I noticed a woman standing off to the side talking to her friend. She was crying. I learned later that her tears were over the fact that she was living in the very condition of physical abuse to which I had referred. Her tears, I was told, were over the fact that this was the first time she had heard the good news and realized that she did not have to stay stuck. I do not know the outcome of the story, whether in fact she found the courage to leave the old for the new. But at least she heard the good news of the gospel as proclaimed in the Beatitudes: be lifted up!

Two Sayings of Jesus: "Turn the other cheek"
and "Give the shirt off your back"

Like the Beatitudes, these particular sayings of Jesus are often understood to mean that we are passively to accept the circumstance or condition in which we might find ourselves. So if someone strikes us, we should take it and turn the other cheek for more! The same is true if someone wants your shirt: not only give them the shirt, but also give them your cloak!

Walter Wink has provided a helpful study of these texts in his book *The Powers that Be*. Placing these texts within the cultural context in which they were written, he shows how these texts were not written to encourage passive submission, but quite the opposite: they were written to tell Jesus' followers that they are no longer to be submissive to the denigrating and berating actions of their masters or of any power that has dominion over them. At the same time, though, neither are they to act violently. They are to be subversively active in taking away the power of the one who dominates! Here is what Wink says of the saying about turning the other cheek:

> The backhand was not a blow to injure, but to insult, humiliate, degrade. It was not administered to an equal, but to an inferior. Masters backhanded slaves; husbands, wives; parents, children; Romans, Jews. The whole point of the blow was to force someone who was out of line back into place.
>
> Notice Jesus' audience: "If anyone strikes *you*." These are people used to being thus degraded. He is saying to them, "Refuse to accept this kind of treatment anymore. If they backhand you, turn the other cheek." By turning the cheek, the servant makes it impossible for the master to use the backhand again; his nose is in the way. And anyway, it's like telling a joke twice if it didn't work the first time, it simply won't work. The left cheek now offers a perfect target for a blow with the right fist; but only equals fought with fists, and as we know from Jewish sources, and the last thing the master wished to do is to establish the underling's equality. This act of defiance renders the master incapable of asserting his dominance in this relationship. He can have the slave beaten, but he can no longer cower him. By turning the cheek, then, the "inferior" is saying: "I'm a human being, just like you. I refuse to be humiliated any longer. I am a child of God. I won't take it anymore."[8]

Regarding the saying about giving one's clothing, Wink says:

---

8. Wink, *The Powers that Be,* 101–2.

Indebtedness was a plague in first-century Palestine. Jesus' parables are full of debtors struggling to salvage their lives. Heavy debt was the direct consequence of Roman imperial policy. Emperors taxed the wealthy heavily to fund their wars. The rich naturally sought non-liquid investments to hide their wealth. Land was best, but it was ancestrally owned and passed down over generations, and no peasant would voluntarily relinquish it. However, exorbitant interest (25 to 250 percent) could be used to drive landowners ever deeper into debt. And debt, coupled with the high taxation required by Herod Antipas to pay Rome tribute, created the economic leverage to pry Galilean peasants loose from their land. By Jesus' time, large estates were owned by absentee landlords, managed by stewards, and worked by tenant farmers, day laborers, and slaves. Jesus' hearers are the poor ("if anyone would sue *you*"). They share a rankling hatred for a system that subjects them to humiliation by stripping them of their lands, their goods, and finally even their outer garments. Why then does Jesus counsel them to give over their undergarments as well? This would mean stripping off all their clothing and marching out of court stark naked! Nakedness was taboo, and shame fell less on the naked party than on the person viewing or causing the nakedness. By stripping, the debtor has brought shame on the creditor. The debtor has not hope of winning the case; the law was entirely in the creditor's favor. But the poor man has transcended this attempt to humiliate him. He has risen above shame. At the same time, he has registered a stunning protest against the system that created his debt. The Powers That Be literally stand on their dignity. Nothing deflates them more effectively than deft

> lampooning. By refusing to be awed by their
> power, the powerless are emboldened to seize
> the initiative, even where structural change is
> not immediately possible.[9]

Like the Beatitudes, these sayings of Jesus are intended to call forth within persons a new understanding of themselves that will lead not only to an inner transformation, but to a new posture and behavior towards the powers that have control over their lives. As Wink observes, these changes in behavior will not lead to an immediate change in the system nor to an immediate reversal of the predicament; however, they do take away the power of the powers that be to make people submit.[10] In fact, resistance to the powers that be may well lead to adverse consequences. But the very act of resisting, rather than passively submitting, is in and of itself a leaving behind what is old for what is new!

John 3:16

There is probably no New Testament text more familiar nor more favored than this one. It is a clear and vivid statement of God's deep compassion for and faithfulness to the creation and creatures the Holy One has made. As well it should be, this text is used time and time again for palliative comfort and support, especially in those moments when one is confronted with the anguish of shame and alienation. At the same time, traditional interpretations and uses of this text tend to isolate these words of

9. Ibid., 103–4.
10. Ibid., 102.

Jesus from the rest of his discourse, thereby rendering them as a statement of God's unconditional acceptance of us. By unconditional acceptance we hear these words mean that God loves and accepts us without any need for change on our part! When coupled with the words that follow, "I did not come to condemn the world," we are comforted and led to believe that everything will be okay, and thus we are allowed to remain in our homeostatic security, even if that "secure" place is not life giving. In operative practices of pastoral care, these words are often used to remind the shamed and guilty of their intrinsic worth and value as human creatures. This is as it should be. Yet the way they are used does not call the hearer forth from what is old into what is new.

What is missing in this interpretation of Jesus' words is the message that immediately follows: "I did not come to condemn, *but I did come for judgment!*" A clear distinction is made between judgment and condemnation. In operative practices of pastoral care, judgment and condemnation are often equated so that the caregiver resists rendering judgment of another for fear of eliciting further shame and guilt. Jesus, on the other hand, makes a clear distinction: I came to bring judgment, but I did not come to condemn! What is this judgment? It is a judgment that reveals the world for what it is. What the world thinks is light is in reality darkness. In Jesus, the truth of the human condition is revealed. When our operative practices of pastoral care leave out this part of the text, we in effect convey the message, "God's love for the world means that we don't have to face the truth."

One way to read these words of Jesus is through the eyes of an intervention: "For God so loved the world that he intervened." Or another reading might be, "For God so loved the world that he told the truth." As already noted, interventions are about confronting someone with the truth of their life so as to help that person initiate change. The truth with which they must be confronted is that the way they are living their life is bringing death and destruction, not only to the individual but to those around him. And here's the catch: *interventions are never conducted with the intent of condemnation.* They are always conducted with the intent of restoring an individual's life. Interventions are acts of love at the deepest level, but they do not feel good for those intervening or for the one intervened upon. They are risky and even dangerous. But they are always acts of love.

Might this not also be so for God's intervention? It comes at great cost for the Holy One who intervenes, but it also comes with cost for those of us being intervened upon, for we must face the truth being revealed. This is painful work! However, in a strange and paradoxical way, this confrontation is really an act of care on the part of the One doing the confronting. When we, as caregivers and leaders, begin to embody this deep and abiding care in our pastoral work, we are moving towards that sort of care and leadership that calls forth new reality.

Mark 16: A Post-Resurrection Appearance of Jesus

Regardless of whether or not Mark 16:9–20 was added by a later editor or is part of the original gospel, it is a remarkable story about the power of resurrection versus the power of fear.[11] The disciples are gathered in the room.

11. Mark 16:9–20 (RSV).

We can easily imagine the scene. They are grieving, perhaps overwhelmed with disbelief and disillusion over the events that have just happened. They have invested themselves in Jesus and believed that following him would reap something other than crucifixion. While not directly mentioned, we can also imagine that with the events of the past few days, the disciples have become abundantly clear about the powers that be and what those power are capable of. Not only are they gathered in disbelief, disillusion, and grief, they are gathered in fear! They are so disheartened—or shall we say so defeated—that they cannot believe the news of the resurrection when it is given them, even by eyewitnesses. Into this scene, the risen Jesus appears. Interestingly, however, he does not appear with words of comfort, nor does he offer any sympathetic understanding for their fear of the powers that threaten them. Instead he outright rebukes them for their inability to see the resurrection when it is right in front of them. In short, Jesus has no sympathy for their emotional state. In fact he is impatient with it, and his impatience is because they are unwilling to claim the power of resurrection for themselves. They are stuck in the room![12]

The author makes a clear distinction between unbelief and belief, between hopelessness and power. Jesus directly challenges the unbelief and helpless attitude of the disciples by saying: "The one who believes has salvation; the one who doesn't believe is condemned." With these words, the reader is challenged not only to believe in the resurrection as something that has physically happened, but more importantly, to claim the power of the resurrec-

---

12. Mark 16:14 (RSV).

tion for one's own life and not be condemned to hopeless and victimized futility.

The writer then concludes this section with Jesus giving a short but direct "farewell speech," one not laden with sentimentality. In effect, he gives the disciples their marching orders. Get out of the room and out into the world. Whoever believes in the resurrection will have power, power over evil and everything that threatens life. Now get out; we've got work to do!

We know the rest of the story! It was their belief in the resurrected Lord, their belief in the power of life over death, that brought them out of the room into the world to challenge the powers that be! It was their belief in the resurrection that moved them from helpless and futile resignation to bold proclamation. It was their belief in the resurrection that moved them from lives of fear to lives of love. Claiming resurrection is neither a cognitive assent to an event that happened, nor is it merely the acceptance of a future life. It is the conviction of what the whole event embodies: death has no power over life. Belief in the reality and power of resurrection is deciding to live in this conviction as opposed to helpless resignation. Resurrection is indeed an existential reality that confronts us at every turn and calls us to leave what is old for what is new.

Elijah and the Cave: 1 Kings 19:1–18

This great story describes the victimization many of us experience in ministry—myself included. Elijah has won the "battle of the prophets." He has commanded the prophets of Baal to be slaughtered. However, when Ahab returns to Jezebel and tells her all that has happened, she is enraged and sends word to Elijah that she will most assuredly kill him! Strangely, after the demonstration of power that has just occurred, Jezebel's threat scares him and he retreats to the wilderness. Coming to a broom tree, he sits down and prays that his life might come to an end.[13]

The prayer sounds futile: "I've had enough! Take my life for it is no better than my ancestors who are already dead." The prayer is answered not with death, but with nourishment for the journey ahead. While Elijah is feeling hopeless about his situation, God is by no means giving in to the threats of Jezebel. So Elijah gets up and travels forty days and forty nights and comes to a cave where he takes refuge. It is here that God's impatience rears its head. God calls out, "Elijah, why are you here?" He answers, "Zeal for your word and doing what you told me to do has gotten me in trouble. I'm the only one left!" Sound familiar? This is victimization at its best![14]

So God calls Elijah out to stand before him on the mountain, and as God passes by, there comes a windstorm, earthquake, and fire. After these displays of power, Elijah hears a small whisper and recognizes it as God's presence. He hides his face. Again, God asks the question: "What are you doing here, Elijah?" And again the victimized response: "Zeal for thy word has gotten me in trouble. Israel has broken all of its covenants, torn down

13. 1 Kings 19:1–4 (RSV).
14. 1 Kings 19:4–10 (RSV).

the altars, killed your prophets, and I am the only one left standing."[15]

One would think that these circumstances deserve sympathetic understanding from God. Yet, nothing of the sort comes. Instead, Elijah is directed to leave the cave and return the way he came. Along the way he is to anoint Hazael to be king of Aram, and Jehu to be king of Israel. In addition Elijah is to anoint Elisha to be his successor. In short, God says to Elijah, "Get out of the cave, we have work to do." While God surely is aware of the powers that threaten Elijah's life, the clear statement in this text is that God will not allow those threats to stand in the way of the work and mission that he has set forth. While remaining in the homeostatic security of the cave would be comfortable, Elijah is called forth to leave and engage the work that has to be done. God does not show sympathetic concern; instead he issues a command and Elijah responds.

Power and Pastoral Care

All of these stories are about power, God's power, and the extent to which that power does not allow for or tolerate stuckness in status quo, homeostatic security. God's power always calls forth new life and new creation, not as an awaited reality, but as a reality that is now and in the moment.

Pastoral care is about living in this new reality so as to claim power over the powers that have control over our lives! It is about claiming our own power, and helping others claim theirs. And herein lies the crux of the mat-

15. 1 Kings 19:11ff. (RSV).

ter simply and succinctly stated: when pastoral caregivers and leaders must face *the powers that be* in whatever form those powers take—family dysfunction, congregational dysfunction, political systems, etc.—we, like Elijah, are often ambivalent about our own power. We find it easier to remain in our homeostatic security than risk entering the struggle! Avoidance is easier and safer than confrontations, challenges, judgments, and naming truths for what they are.

This is not simply a psychological issue, nor one that can simply be understood by looking at our genograms, although these are important and extremely helpful, as we shall later see. There is a theological reason for our ambivalence: it is an implicit and explicit belief that understands God as an endlessly sympathetic caretaker rather than as one who is relentlessly calling us forth to leave behind what is old for what is new even if that transformation means discomfort, anxiety, and dis-ease.

Our images do not include the God who is girded for battle against the powers that be or anything else that seeks to wrest life away from what the creating God intended. This is a God who is passionate, tenacious, determined, and wants us to be the same regardless of the power that holds our life. Just as God is engaged, so God wants us to be engaged! This is how God loves us!

Douglas John Hall observes that our culture's understanding and use of the phrase, "God is love," "is frequently a dubious blend of sentimentality and pietism."[16] He goes on to say: "And if the cross of Jesus Christ is the apex of God's definition of God's love, then the divine love

16. Hall, *The Cross in our Context*, 78.

has very little to do with the 'luv' that is passed around so liberally in our contemporary context."[17] The God of "luv" is the God who is filtered through our cultural images, which means that we understand God's love as an emotion. This is the God who leaves us feeling good, the God who never challenges or calls forth. This is the God who is looking after me and gently holding me through whatever circumstance I might be in. For Hall, the God of love is the God to whom we have referred throughout this discussion, the God who is never content to let the created order fall into the hands of the powers that be, the God who is engaged and always calling forth new life out of old chaos.

The more I read the Scriptures, the more I become aware of the extent to which belief in this God of love will not allow resignation. God is a God of life who is calling us forth to participate in new life and new reality here and now. God is calling us forth to stand against the powers that be wherever those powers are trying to take away life. Pastoral care and leadership, if it is to embody this God of deep care and compassion, means not only standing with and beside anyone who is facing those powers in their life circumstance, it is also to speak prophetically so that those to whom care is being offered will begin to hear God's calling forth.

I conclude this chapter with a brief story that illustrates what this sort of pastoral care looks like. During my tenure at the Lutheran Seminary Program in the Southwest, we created an intensive language program that required our students to attend three weeks of language

17. Ibid.

and cultural immersion at the CETLALIC language school in Cuernavaca, Mexico. Not only were students required to attend the structured language classes at the school, they were also required to live with home-stay families as a way of learning both culture and language. Having participated in this experience several times, I can attest to the fact that is an incredibly challenging and at times even daunting experience. As an alternative language school, CETLALIC not only teaches its students Spanish language and Mexican culture, but it is also committed to raising students' awareness of the social, political, and economic realities of Mexican life, particularly as those realities are affected and impacted by the wealth and politics of the United States. So the challenge of CETLALIC is not only about being in a strange and foreign place and having to learn the language and culture to survive; it is about having one's eyes and mind opened to the realities of poverty, injustice, and oppression and the extent to which United States wealth and politics have contributed to those conditions. In short, it is not an easy experience.

This is a true story of a student and his wife who, upon realizing how challenging and even discomforting the experience was going to be, decided to leave. The host family were elderly people, yet highly respected and revered within the CETLALIC community. They were faithful Roman Catholics who were active in the base community movement. When the student and his wife decided to leave, they did not at first tell their hostess. She eventually found out from the housing coordinator at the language school. When she did find out, she did not sit idly by, nor did she offer sympathetic understanding. Instead she called for a meeting with the student and his wife. Knowing that he was a minister, she began the meeting, "They tell me you are a minister. Perhaps we should look at what is going on by having a Bible study."

Being active in the base community movement, this "uneducated" woman knew something about using the reflection method of study. She began the Bible study by reading the story of Jesus walking on water and Peter trying to do the same yet unable to do so because he recognizes and gives in to his fear. I do not know the details of how the conversation went in that reflection. I can only imagine. However, in and through this reflective study, this incredible woman helped the student and his wife recognize that they were like Peter. They had given in to the power of their fear! More challenging and discomforting to them was the recognition of the discrepancy between their professed faith and their behavior. As the story goes, they recognized the challenge of their hostess and they remained at the school as discomforting and disorienting as it was. In doing so we can assume that they were able to leave their stuckness for what appears to have been a life-giving experience.

This brief vignette is an excellent illustration of the pastoral care that emerges when the caregiver's position is one of power and not sympathetic protection. In this story the caregiver's goal is not to help the recipient of care feel good, nor is it to relieve his anxiety. The caregiver in this instance knows very well what the recipients of her care were up against. In fact she knew more about what power was at work than they did, and in the face of that power, she refused to back down. Rather than say, "Well, I'm sorry this hasn't worked for you," she instead called a meeting and initiated a Bible study. She was not ambivalent about her power. She recognized the power at work in the student and his wife, and she realized the consequences if they are allowed to give in to that power. She therefore intervened! She did not take care of them, but neither was she rude or condemning. By inviting them into the Scriptures, she challenged them to look at their reality and to identify the power with which they are contending. Most importantly, she called forth in them a new reality that transcends their fear. With this calling forth, they were left to decide whether they wanted to be victims and remain stuck, or to leave the old for something new.

If we believe that God is a God who is always creating and calling the human creature out of the old into the new, then the work of pastoral care is about this business of calling forth and leading, helping and assisting people leave what is old and venture into what is new. It is about helping people muster the courage to leave behind whatever it is that holds them captive and wrests their life away. It is about helping them find the courage and strength to stay the course when they want to return to the security of what they have left. As this story attests, the ability to carry out this work is not about learning new techniques and methods. Rather, it is about gaining deeper clarity and awareness about our fundamental calling when we encounter and engage the powers that be. In the next chapter, we turn to that challenge.

Questions for Discussion and Reflection

1. Reflect on your practice of pastoral care and leadership. What are the prevailing biblical narratives that have shaped your understanding of your pastoral office, your pastoral identity, and your practice of ministry?

2. Reflecting on your ministry, what characteristics of God are most embodied in your care and leadership?

3. What "powers that be" do you come up against most in your ministry? What position do you find yourself taking when you face these powers? Working towards consensus? Avoidance? Sympathetic protection? Confrontation? How do your images of God influence and shape the position you take?

4. What are your reactions to the biblical narratives (and their interpretations) presented in this chapter? What new insight or awareness (if any) do they give you about your pastoral care and leadership?

5. What are your reactions to the idea that God's love and care is offered from the position of power, not sympathetic understanding or protection? What implications does this have for your practice of ministry and the way you embody God's love and care?

Three

Called to Care—But It Might Not Be What You Thought

The Expectation of Ministry
versus the Experience of Ministry

As with anyone entering a new career, pastors and candidates for ordination enter their practice with assumptions and expectations. Persons entering ministry expect to be good pastors. They expect to be effective care-givers and leaders. They have expectations of how they will do the work of ministry, how they will lead, and what they will offer or say to people. They have expectations of how their ministry will be received, and at deeper levels, they have expectations of the satisfaction and reward they will receive for having offered themselves in ministry. Many persons entering ministry expect to find an inner peace and satisfaction for the care and comfort they will offer hurting people. This is as it should be. These expectations are what drive us and give us hope. At the same time, expectations usually clash with experience: things aren't what we thought they would be.[1] Ministry does not turn out as one had hoped. These moments of disillusionment can be painful and often conflicted. The effect one had hoped to have on others and the world does not come about. The community of faith is not the environment of warmth and love as one had imagined; on the contrary it is often found to be hostile. The inner satisfaction and peace one thought would be found does not occur; instead ministry is found to be a constant source of tension. In short, persons in ministry discover that it is not the idealized world they had imagined. To be more specific, they discover that ministry does not change anything about their life as they had hoped. They are still the same persons they were before they entered the practice, and they carry the same baggage they did before they entered ministry. And like it or not, they also discover that the world of the church is no different than the rest of the world. It is still made up of human beings, and it is a community that despite its claims often lives like the rest of the world. More than anything else, however, the most disillusioning moment for pastors occurs when we discover that we are not the "good pastors" we had hoped to be; our niceness, our attempts to offer care and comfort, our unconditional acceptance of others do not produce the results we had envisioned. We are surprised when we find ourselves at the center of conflict and turmoil, often unaware of how our desire and good intentions could turn into such a mess.

When pastors arrive at these moments where expectations clash with experience, it is often the case that they

1. Hall, *Lighten Our Darkness*, 19.

find themselves stuck, unable to offer effective pastoral care or leadership. In systems thinking, we find ourselves working harder and harder doing the same thing over and over to no avail. A brief vignette will illustrate my point. Several years ago, the pastor and staff of a large congregation in a metropolitan community came to the Ministry Development Center for a staff consultation. They were navigating difficult circumstances having initiated changes in the life and direction of the congregation, and the senior pastor in particular was the target of significant criticism. They came seeking some sort of "answer" about how to get through it all. As the consultation unfolded, it became clear that the pastor was shouldering considerable responsibility for the anxiety and dis-ease being felt by many of the congregants. As he put it, "I feel like all I can do is stay hunkered down in the foxhole to avoid the fire." Stuckness cannot be more aptly described! Through the course of the consultation, the entire staff became aware of its "foxhole behavior" and the paralysis that resulted. The real crux of the matter, however, was not in the pastor's self-protective behavior. It was in his recognition that the love and care he was extending to his critics were unable to change their behavior. Even more significant was the realization that the love and care he was extending to his critics were enabling their behavior because it was void of any challenge to their reactivity. As the pastor reflected on these dynamics and how he was contributing to the problem, he also became aware of the extent to which his behavior was shaped by his expectations of himself in ministry. In short, his expectation was: "If I'm nice enough and love people enough, I will be able to effect change in them and the congregation."

Moreover, his belief was that in and through this niceness and love, he would receive the affirmation and satisfaction for which he yearned. Thus, as difficulties and conflicts mounted, the pastor along with his staff continued to work harder and harder at their niceness, trying to win folks over through unconditional affirmation and love. Yet nothing changed until all they could do was retreat to the foxhole.

If we unpack this vignette further, we recognize an assumption that most of us bring to our ministry practice: loving our congregants does not include challenge, confrontation, or calling forth new reality when non-life-giving behavior erupts. For this pastor, loving congregants meant unconditional affirmation even when they were doing destructive things. It did not include the calling forth of new reality such as the setting of boundaries; it did not include calling them forth to function at a different level of behavior that might contribute to more effective community life. His stuckness, though, was not due to lack of skill or competency. It was the result of the fact that he was functioning out of a set of assumptions and expectations of what it means to be a good and caring pastor. Those assumptions and expectations did not allow for him to take a differentiated stand that would challenge the disruptive and even demonic behavior of his detractors and call forth a new way of being.

Like this pastor, most of us come into ministry with the expectation that we will be good pastors. We expect that in and through the work of ministry we will do good things and be good persons. To be sure, doing and being good means different things for different people, but in general the expectation of finding our goodness in the work of ministry is quite similar to the pastor in the vignette: if we love, care for, and are nice enough to those we serve, we will win the day. Cognitively, we know this not to be true, and most pastors I know would deny that they believe it for themselves. Yet emotionally, this is the formula by which many in ministry define themselves and it is the truth out of which many of us unwittingly function. Thus, when we are stuck and find ourselves at the I-don't-know-what-else-to-do moment, I submit that the powers we are up against are not external. They are internal and they are our own assumptions and expectations of what it means to be a good pastor. In short, our old ways of doing and being good are not working, but like most, we do not search for new ways to define ourselves: rather we simply adapt, working harder and harder at doing the same old things until we can do nothing but retreat to the foxhole.

But where do these assumptions and expectations come from? Who or what has told us that good pastors are those who take care of people and don't challenge bad behavior? Who or what has told us that good pastoral leaders provide answers rather than ask questions? Who or what has told us that good pastors are supposed to make us feel good rather than challenge us to rise to the occasion? In this regard, Friedman's analysis is helpful, and to that analysis we now turn.

Leadership in a Regressive Society: Working Hard to Be Good

Friedman observed ours to be a society that has gone into emotional regression, the result of which is an environment that mightily resists differentiated leadership.[2] Leaders who see the bigger picture of our problems and realize that getting out of them will require difficult and courageous change are usually sabotaged. They are often ousted in favor of those who will offer quick fixes, easy answers, and above all, the immediate relief of anxiety and dis-ease. The hallmark of the regressed society is its diminished capacity to rise to the occasion to meet the challenge of change.

My observation is that this diminished capacity is not simply a desire for good feelings. It is much deeper. It's as if there is an underlying belief that associates goodness with the absence of dis-ease, discomfort, struggle, or pain of any sort. It is a rather short and succinct formula: we have arrived at goodness and we are good when we are free of struggle, pain, discomfort or dis-ease; we are failures when we are not in this state of being. Life, then, is the pursuit of this state of goodness. This is the belief at the heart of the American Dream and the pursuit of happiness. We are not just pursuing a state of bliss for its own sake; we are pursuing the deeper state of goodness that the feeling of happiness and contentment represent. And herein lies the catch: by associating feelings of happiness, contentment, and bliss with goodness, we delude ourselves into believing we have arrived at goodness when we feel good, even if those feelings have been self-induced through non-life-giving means to cover up the truth that things are not good. I'm not referring here to what we usually associate with delusion, like drugs, alcohol, or sex addictions. Rather, think of individuals and families

2. Friedman, *Failure of Nerve*, 53.

who truly believe they have attained goodness through their wealth, status, or materialism, even though considerable dysfunction, pain, and suffering are underneath the facade. Think of individuals and families who truly believe they have arrived at happiness and peace—hence goodness—through their religion, yet underneath their religious mask lies the pain of insecurity, loneliness, hurt, abandonment, and shame. Think of families who associate their goodness with being "one big happy family" free of conflict. They may be aware of the dis-ease and discontent that exists within their family unit, yet they work hard to keep those feelings underground in order to appear united and together. Goodness is intrinsically tied to everyone being happy and together even if that is not the reality. Associating goodness with the absence of dis-ease, discomfort, struggle, and pain leads to a false pursuit. Worse yet, it associates the engagement and acknowledgment of these painful realities with failure and shame. When the truths of these sorts of realities are allowed to come to light, it is not just that we have failed; we *are* failures. No wonder then that we must work so hard at the pursuit of feeling good, for when we *feel good we believe ourselves to be good.*

This pursuit of goodness takes place in organizations and congregations as well. Just like individuals, congregations believe they will attain goodness when they have achieved certain markers in their life. To be sure, it may not be the happiness or contentment that individuals seek, but it is very much related. The feeling that seems most associated with goodness in congregations is security. Just like other organizational systems, congregations strive for security, and that security comes when it sees outward marks of success, increased membership, high levels of giving and stable finances, well-manicured facilities that include state of the art media technology, and of course the dynamite youth program that attracts children and teenagers from all over town. Like individuals and families, they believe they will have attained security and goodness when they can be "one big happy family" free of conflict and discord. Some of my work at the Ministry Development Center included consultation with congregations and congregational leaders. A consistent theme among them was the insecurity they felt because they were not "succeeding" in the same way as the mega-church down the street. Their children and youth were leaving for other congregations that were more fun and exciting. They could not attract new members because they didn't have an exciting and vibrant worship style. The list could go on, but at the heart of it all was a deep and abiding fear that they were dying, and if they were to die they would fail. More to the point, if they were to die, they would be failures.

Whether we are talking about individuals, families, congregations, or organizations, all live with the deep-seated belief that they will attain goodness when they achieve or arrive at certain defined markers. It is a pursuit driven by the chronic fear of failing. The notions of goodness and failure that drive this pursuit, however, are not inherent in creation and the life process. In the first creation story we read that at the end of each day, God took note that what had been created was good, indeed very good![3] Nowhere do we read that the goodness of

3. Genesis 1:1–2:3 (RSV).

the created order or the goodness of the human creature was contingent upon achieving certain defined markers. Goodness was inherent in creation, and it did not need to be achieved or pursued. Somewhere along the way our notions of what is good and how we attain goodness deviated from what was intended. Of course there is another story in Genesis that speaks to this deviation, and we might say that human creatures have been defining good and striving for goodness on their own terms ever since.[4] Our chronic fear of failure and our incessant striving for goodness through non-life-giving means are rooted in the ancient stories of creation and fall.

It doesn't take long to see how this belief and the resulting pursuit of goodness impacts leadership and caregiving. We want leaders and caregivers who will help us attain the markers we associate with goodness: happiness, contentment, absence of discord, security, and the list goes on. We want leaders and caregivers who will help us achieve goodness in our old familiar ways, even if those old familiar ways aren't working and are contributing to the perpetuation of a chronic condition. Is it any wonder that our current political system is so bankrupt and failing? One simply cannot get elected if one offers a long-term solution that requires fundamental change in our way of life or requires the electorate to rise to the occasion and make courageous sacrifices. We want leaders and caregivers who do not challenge us to face the truths and realities of life that would cause us discomfort, affliction, or anxiety. We want caregivers and leaders who offer us quick solutions and remedies rather than those who

4. Genesis 3:1–24 (RSV).

would stand in front and lead us through the difficult changes that are needed. In short, we want leaders and caregivers who will adapt to our adaptivity. We want leaders and caregiver who will support our misguided beliefs and pursuits of goodness that are driven by our chronic fear of failure.

Friedman observed that this adaptivity has given rise to three prevailing myths: the myth of data and information, the myth of empathy, and the myth of self.[5] As we shall see in what follows, all of these operate in some form or fashion in pastoral caregivers and leaders.

The Myth of Data—Finding Goodness in Getting it Right

The myth of data and information simply stated is the belief that the more information and data we have, the better and more effective leaders we will become. The advance of technology and the impact of the availability of information on how we function in society is no secret. Friedman observes, however, that these advances are not the reason for our excessive dependence on information. He says, "It is societal regression, first by perverting the natural instincts of curiosity and adventure into a dogged quest for certainty, and second by focusing on pathology rather than strength."[6] I suggest that the "dogged quest for certainty," and the "focusing on pathology rather than strength" are both related to the pursuit of goodness. Both are aimed at "getting it right," which as we have already seen is deeply rooted in the chronic fear of failing.

5. Friedman, *Failure of Nerve,* 95–186.
6. Ibid., 97.

The chronic anxiety of getting it right is often at the heart of many church conflicts, whether in congregations, synods, or church-wide organizations. The anxiety of failing—particularly if persons believe they will have failed in the eyes of God when "they get it wrong"—drives many to search for the exact answer to a predicament or to become fearful of those they perceive to be leading in wrong directions. I once saw this evident in a denominational judicatory's committee on ordination that had asked me to consult with them on how they might better assess persons' readiness for ordination. My presentation focused on what I continue to believe is a truth: when all is said and done, the matter of determining a person's readiness for ministry is subjective. There are no objective or structured processes given in Scripture. When the community needs to determine who its leaders will be or who it is calling into a particular task or work, it comes together for a conversation. It prays for the Spirit to be present and to give the gathered body a mind and spirit out of which a collective wisdom will prevail. I went on to suggest that the little phrase in the Acts of the Apostles might be our best guide: "It seems good to us and the Spirit." My point was simply that when a committee on ordination comes together and engages in this kind of conversation, it already has what it needs to make its determination. To be sure, there are resources and instruments that help with the process, but in the end, the collective wisdom of the gathered body is likely to be its best tool. I was taken aback by the strong reaction of one group in the committee who wanted more stringent measurements. As it turned out, the issues around which this committee had long been divided and gridlocked, came to the fore. I soon found out that this particular group wanted ordination candidates to be able to give the correct answers to certain questions and markers, such as whether or not they adhered to a particular method of biblical interpretation, and whether or not they were against ordaining gays and lesbians and same-sex marriages. My presentation was derailed and I found it difficult to navigate the conflict that erupted. In hindsight, I realized that the reactivity manifested by these particular committee members was rooted in their fear of failing. To allow persons of liberal persuasions into ministry was in their mind to have failed God. They were focused on what they considered to be the "pathology" of the church, a failure that needed correcting. Their way of making these corrections was to find sure and certain answers that would determine which candidates were qualified and which ones weren't.

The search for certainty takes place in other ways as well, and it is not limited to those who are more conservative or who are trying to save the church from what they perceive are its moral failings. When faced with the task of providing pastoral care to persons in very difficult circumstances and crises, students and pastors with all levels of experience will often ask, "What's the right thing to say?" The question and comment reveals their underlying anxiety: a deep fear of *not getting it right*. The fear of not getting it right brings on such a paralysis that the caregiver loses the ability to bring his own heart, imagination, and creativity to bear in the moment. In an effort to *get it right*, the caregiver looks outside of himself for the *right answer*. It's as if there is this body of knowledge "out there" that has the magical answer. Underneath this search is the unspoken belief that "I don't have what it takes to be a good pastor in this circumstance because I don't have enough knowledge or expertise." From the very outset, the focus is on what the pastor doesn't have as opposed to what she does have. The focus is on weakness, not strength. Yet it is often the case that when the caregiver explores her life history, she discovers that she has had some experience that gives her a body of knowledge about the circumstance to which she is being called to give care. It is a knowledge born out of her life experience, yet a knowledge that somehow has not been given credence. To be sure, it may not yet be honed into the kind of effectiveness that she is looking for, but it is a body of knowledge nonetheless, and it is worthy of being called expert knowledge.

The chronic fear of failing and the quest to "get things right" also manifests itself in preaching. Consistent with what Friedman has said about the regressive society, parishioners seem to want more answers than questions from their preachers. *It is as if we have redefined faith to mean certainty rather than trust.* So, we expect preachers to give us certain and right answers to whatever predicaments we face, and we want those answers given in manageable sound bytes. The expert answer sought is one that will bring chaos and anxiety under control, clarity to ambiguity, certainty to uncertainty, and answers to questions. It is no wonder that so many pastors find themselves feeling inadequate in their preaching. When they work hard to meet these expectations they find themselves coming up short every time.

Congregations, likewise, tend to focus on weaknesses rather than strengths and thereby look for answers outside of themselves. When confronted with a predicament, problem, or new challenge, most believe they need to call in the experts. It is as if someone "out there" will have the right answer to the predicament or situation, an answer they don't believe they have the capacity to imagine or create! The same fear of failure that takes hold of caregivers and leaders takes hold of congregations.

Whether as individuals, families, congregations or organizations, nothing has the ability to rob us of the expertise, power, and goodness that we already posses as does this fear! We are so afraid of failing that we get stuck trying to find right answers outside of ourselves. This fear is so powerful that it robs us of the God given ability to imagine and create new answers, new solutions and— God forbid—new ways of thinking! The fear of failing is what drives us to the foxhole!

The Myth of Empathy—Finding Goodness in Keeping Everyone Happy and Together

The myth of empathy might be more aptly called the myth of sympathetic protection or the myth of keeping everything together and peaceful. This myth—like the myth of expertise—is also directly connected to the chronic fear of failing. When conflict or dis-ease finds its way into a congregation or family, understanding and sympathetic protection are often employed to avoid the pain of change and to keep the system together, even if it means the perpetuation of a chronic condition. An example of what I'm talking about can be found in a family that was a member of a congregation I once served. The oldest of two children in this particular family engaged in behavior that continued to get him in trouble. Time and time again his mother would rescue him from the situation, sometimes in ways the other family members didn't know about. Her rescuing began to dwindle her small inheritance until the second child intervened and asked the mother to change her enabling behavior. The mother steadfastly refused and the chronic condition continued. At the heart of the mother's refusal to change was a deep and abiding fear of failure. Had she shifted her position in the system so as to allow her son to reap the consequences of his behavior, there would have been public consequences. The fusion between the two was so deep that his failure would have been her failure, a failure she could not bear. In addition, a shift in position would have undoubtedly resulted in her son directing intense anger towards her, an anger that would have represented failure on her part. More devastating was the threat that he would leave the family if she did not relieve him from his predicament. Nothing would have communicated her failure more than his emotional cut off.

More interesting in this situation was not only her refusal to change, but how she employed understanding and sympathetic protection to avoid change. Rather than challenge this adult child to take responsibility for himself, she expressed understanding and sympathy for his situation, chastising others in the family for not doing the same. After all, she would say, "He's different and we have to understand that." There it is! All of a sudden the most disruptive person in the system becomes the one who is most deserving of the family's sympathetic understanding because this person has a problem to which everyone else must acquiesce and adapt, regardless of how destructive that problem is to the rest of the system.

It is the same with pastors and congregations. Knowing a chronic condition in a congregation needs changing, knowing persons in the congregation who are doing destructive things need to be challenged, pastors and congregations refuse to do so for fear that the one causing the problem will somehow be upset, or worse yet, leave. What is there about us that causes us to put up with such destructive behavior, and in fact enable it through excessive understanding and sympathy? Like the mother, it is our fear of failure. Somehow we have been infected with the insidious belief that we have failed when others act out and manipulate us, and along the way our immunity and capacity to withstand this fatal infection has greatly diminished. Our fear of failure has given rise to a misguided understanding and niceness that do nothing but perpetuate the chronic conditions that destroy life.

The Myth of Self—Finding Goodness in False Humility

Like the myths of expertise and keeping everyone happy, the myth of self is also rooted in the fear of failure. We might also refer to this myth as the myth of false humility. Good leaders and caregivers are those who follow the example of Jesus by "denying themselves," a term that has come to mean keeping one's own convictions, beliefs, values, visions, dreams, wishes, desires, and hopes under wrap so that others can have their way and say, even when their way and say is destructive. To deny one's self is to give up one's voice. We know what happens to pastors when they step out of this model and begin to evidence a more differentiated leadership:

> They are described as compulsive rather than persistent, as obsessive rather than committed, as foolhardy rather than brave, as dreamers rather than imaginative, as single-minded rather than dedicated, as inflexible rather than principled, as hostile rather than aggressive, as bull-headed rather than resolute, as desperate rather than inspired, as autocratic rather than tough-minded, as ambitious rather than courageous, as domineering rather than self-confident, as egotistical rather than self-assured, as selfish rather than self-possessed—and as insensitive, callous, and cold rather than determined.[7]

Friedman goes on to say that this sort of "sabotage will be cloaked by supposed virtues like safety and togetherness."[8] I suggest that when pastors are thus sabotaged it is with the cloak of humility: the pastor is simply not being the humble pastor he is supposed to be.

Within the Christian tradition, it doesn't take long to realize what has given rise to this false humility. Jesus said loud and clear, "Deny yourself and take up the cross." Taking up the cross means endure the suffering but do not stand up or assert yourself. And of course this attitude gains more traction with Jesus' words, "If anyone strikes you, let them strike the other cheek." Somewhere along the way, our interpretations of these texts have given rise to the idea that humility in the tradition of Jesus means putting aside one's self for the sake of everyone else, especially in times of conflict and criticism. A good example of how this false humility works is seen in a pastor with whom I was consulting. Her predicament was that within

7. Ibid., 161–62.
8. Ibid.

71

a group whose work she was leading and facilitating certain dynamics had developed that were destructive to the group's process and were sabotaging her leadership. When asked why she wasn't establishing clearer boundaries, her response was, "For me, boundaries are bad! They make me look like I am selfish." The myth of self could not be more aptly illustrated. As in this case, humility as we have come to understand and practice it means giving up one's own power and integrity and letting others have theirs. More destructive still is the idea that good pastors are those who do not set boundaries for themselves and are willing to sacrifice their spiritual, emotional, and physical health—not to mention their families—for the sake of everyone else. In short good pastors do not assert their power!

In my CPE supervisory practice, I have observed students as they discover their self and begin to find ways of using that self in their ministry practice. More often than not they will say, "I grew up hearing and believing that the self was bad, that somehow if I give credence to it, I am doing something wrong and even sinful." This sort of comment cuts right to the heart of the matter. What has evolved is something more than not trusting our own thoughts, beliefs, visions, dreams, hopes and aspirations. It is an emotional climate that tells us there is something fundamentally wrong with us—yes, even in the eyes of God—if we dare assert our self in any kind of way. And so the fear of failure that prevents us from asserting our self is more than a fear of not getting it right; it is a deep and pervasive fear that we will be judged guilty by God of the sin of pride.

Isn't it strange that the very one who gave us these words about denying self and turning the other cheek was never shy about speaking his mind? Nor was he shy about going into the most sacred of places to turn the tables and chastise the religious powers that be for their misuse of the tradition. As we saw in chapter 2, the verses and texts that have traditionally been used to perpetuate the myth of humility—the Beatitudes, the sayings of Jesus about turning the other cheek and the cloak off your back—are actually about living in and with a new kind of dignity, strength, and integrity. They are not stories that tell the hearer to "roll over and take it," as many have suggested. Quite the opposite. They are stories that encourage the hearer to stand up and let it be known that their integrity and dignity cannot be taken away by any power.

By now, the reader will get the drift of my argument: when these three myths are operative in our ministry practice, they are indicators of our pursuit to be the good leaders and caregivers we want and expect ourselves to be. Yet the irony is that the more we allow these myths to undergird our work, and the harder we work to help those we serve find immediate relief from their anxiety and dis-ease—in short, feel good—we sacrifice our personal integrity and the integrity of our vocational calling. And yes, when these myths are operative in our ministry practices, we will eventually find ourselves in the condition of stuck!

Without question, pastors and caregivers are called to care for and about those who have been entrusted to them. We are called to be good stewards of our gifts and graces, and we are called to be good and to do good work. However, when faced with the realization that we are trying to achieve goodness in old familiar ways that are only getting us stuck, we are faced with a *kairos* moment. It is a moment of opportunity to do the internal work to which we referred in the first chapter. It is an opportunity to redefine our notions of what it means to be good and redefine our vocational calling. If we engage this opportunity and avail ourselves to this inner work of redefinition, we may be surprised to find that doing and being good might not be what we thought!

Rethinking What it Means to be a Good Pastor through the Lens of Luther's Theology of the Cross

An important resource to help us reframe what it means to be a good and caring pastor is found in Luther's theology of the cross. In the *Heidelberg Disputation* and the *Commentary on the Magnificat*, as in other writings, Luther makes the distinction between a theology of the cross and a theology of glory.[9] It should be said at the outset that when Luther speaks about a theology of the cross or a theology of glory, he is not merely speaking about a cognitive way of conceptualizing God. For Luther, a theology of the cross and a theology of glory are *ways of life*. They are two very different ways of seeing God in the world and two different ways of defining one's self in relationship to God and neighbor. They are ways of seeing God and ourselves that will be reflected in our attitudes, values, and behavior in the world.

9. Luther, *The Heidelberg Disputation*, 39–69, and *The Magnificat*, 297–355.

For Luther, a theology of the cross is always a theology of paradox and opposites. God is present and at work in the very places in which God seems most absent or in places that do not have any appearance or semblance of what our senses perceive as God. God is hidden in the depths of our humanity and human experience—in suffering, death, and cross and in whatever forms those take. A theology of glory, on the other hand, looks for God in places that appear to our senses as god-like: places of success, triumph, and power. A theology of the cross trusts God and God's goodness to be present in human experience, however frightful or despairing that experience may be. A theology of the glory, on the other hand, cannot trust one's humanness or human experience as the place where God is revealed. In a theology of glory, anything human must be transcended in order to attain God and goodness.

Another way we might make the distinction is that a theology of glory is always about pretense, illusion, and deception. It avoids at all costs the truths and realities of what it means to be human. A theology of glory cannot fathom the idea that the holy and sacred are to be found in what is ordinary, mundane, tainted, and even sinful. Life in a theology of glory is always a pursuit to deny or transcend one's humanness. A theology of the cross, on the other hand, is a theology of truth. It is a way of life that does not lie or live in pretense about the human condition, regardless of what that condition might be. It does not give in to self deceptions and illusions. In the Heidelberg Disputation, Luther puts it this way: "A theology of glory calls evil good and good evil. A theology of the cross calls the thing what it actually is!"[10]

Unlike a theology of glory, a theology of the cross engages the human condition and human experience, not as something to be conquered or overcome. Indeed, as Luther points out on more than one occasion, the truth of the human condition is that it is full of evil, sin, and death. Yet paradoxically, from the standpoint of a theology of the cross the magnitude of such sinfulness is in no way reason for one to avoid his humanness or his human experience. Hidden in all of this human mess is God and God's goodness, bringing forth life out of death, light out of darkness, hope out of despair. From the vantage point of a theology of the cross, we do not find God by searching the heavens. No. We find God by looking into or own human experience of suffering, death, and cross. This is how Luther states it in the Heidelberg Disputation:

- That person does not deserve to be called a theologian who looks upon the invisible things of God as though they were clearly perceptible in those things which have actually happened.

- He deserves to be called a theologian, however, who comprehends the visible and manifest things of God seen through suffering and the cross.[11]

Thus a theology of the cross turns the tables on everything. One can readily see that a theology of the cross does not provide immediate relief of anxiety. It does not remove disquieting and discomforting feelings. It does not remove pain or suffering in any way. More emphatically, a

10. Luther, *The Heidelberg Disputation*, 53.
11. Ibid., 52.

theology of the cross calls us to sit in these moments with no pretense or illusion about their reality nor about the power they have over our life. A theology of the cross calls us to be in these moments acknowledging our weakness, albeit not as helpless victims. Paradoxically, a theology of the cross calls us to be in these moments with a sure and certain hope that goodness—God's goodness—is deeply present, alive, and at work bringing forth life, hidden and veiled though it might be. A theology of the cross does not offer palliative comfort! It simply offers the strange paradox that our power in these moments is in our weakness, our life is in our dying, our light is in our darkness. God's good and creating activity is at work precisely in the moment where it is hidden and veiled from the naked eye and human ways of knowing.

In the example of the pastor who thought setting boundaries was a bad and selfish thing, her false humility was actually an attempt to transcend her humanness and her human experience of anger. Paradoxically, her anger and power would have served her leadership and the group process quite well, yet she could not trust that goodness might be hidden in what she thought was bad, or that they might actually be the place where God's work could unfold. To be sure, anger and power have enormous potential for evil, and because of her history, she had good reason to be afraid of them. But that is exactly the paradox of a theology of the cross: in what appears bad and evil to our senses, there God's good is hidden. By denying these aspects of her person and keeping them at bay, and by putting away her power and authority in order to be nice and achieve peace in the group she was actually attempting to derive goodness on her terms. Although it had the veneer of humility and self sacrifice—all marks of the cross—it was actually a theology of glory. A theology of the cross, on the other hand, would have invited her to trust the very human things within her that she felt were bad: her anger and her power. Moreover, a theology of the cross would have invited her to trust the chaos and dis-ease that would have resulted had she confronted the group's dysfunction rather than clean it up and make it look nice. A theology of the cross would have invited her to trust the messy human experience of anger and conflict as the place where God is at work, even though it would have been impossible to comprehend God's presence in the midst of such mess! Most of us are no different than this pastor. We find it difficult to trust that the very things within our humanness that scare us the most might actually have potential to be our best gifts for ministry.

Indeed, the theology of the cross turns everything inside out and upside down. Goodness and the pursuit of doing good are seen through a new set of lens. What we think is bad might actually be good; what we think is good might actually be bad. Let us return to Friedman's three myths to look more closely at how this reordering of goodness might change things.

As we have seen, the myth of expertise is really about finding the right answers to ensure certainty. It is driven by our fear of failing, and the result is a paralysis that does not allow us to take risks. Good pastoral leaders and caregivers are those who play it safe by making sure that they have all of the correct data, all of the expert answers before venturing out. If a theology of the cross turns the tables and redefines good, might it be that the good pastoral leader and caregiver is not the one who has all of the expert answers, but actually the one who trusts her heart and encourages her congregants to trust theirs so that they are willing to take courageous risks and ventures, even into uncertain futures that might bring failure. Might it be that the good pastoral leader and caregiver is not the one who resolves problems with answers of certainty, but rather the one who leads others into their ambiguity and unknowing! Might it also be that the good pastoral caregiver and leader is the one who helps others stop searching for right answers outside of themselves, encouraging them to trust that the answers for which they are searching might already be in their own heart, imagination, and creativity. Perhaps more than anything, might it be that the good pastoral leader and caregiver is the one who encourages others—whether individuals, congregations, or organizations—to risk failing! Even more radical is the idea that the good pastor might be the one who not only has given himself the freedom to fail, but in actual circumstances has ventured out, taken risks, entered into ambiguity and unknowing, and has in fact failed. Yes, it is a radical idea to be sure!

In the myth of empathy or sympathetic protection, goodness is derived from protecting an individual or organization from the truth of its condition. The projection of the illusion that all is well when it isn't, is in reality a theology of glory. The mother who protected her son from the consequences of his destructive behavior was functioning out of a theology of glory. Pastors who protect their congregations from the truths of the congregation's chronic conditions are living in a theology of glory along with their congregations. If a theology of the cross turns the tables, might it be that the good pastoral leader and caregiver (or parent) is the one who names the condition for what it is and does not attempt to rescue anyone from the consequences of it. Had the mother allowed the son "to die," and suffer the consequences of his behavior, she would have appeared on the surface as a bad parent. Yet it would have been the most loving and caring thing she could have done, indeed a good thing. Pastors who allow their congregants or congregations "to die" in the same way will appear on the surface as bad and unsuccessful pastors, yet helping individuals or organizations die in order that they can have life may well be the most caring thing that can happen.

In the myth of self, as we have seen, good pastors are those who practice humility by denying their thoughts, feelings, hopes and dreams, and defer to others. Another way of saying it is that good and caring pastors are those who give up their power so that others can exercise theirs. Often that sacrifice of power means letting others dictate the direction of their ministry rather than letting that direction be charted by their own vocational call. If a theology of the cross turns the tables on this false—and yes, idolatrous—piety, then the good and caring pastor might actually be the one who risks appearing strong willed by standing on her convictions, yet staying connected to her adversaries in the height of their reactivity. The good and caring pastor might be the one who risks appearing as uncaring when not giving into demands for sympathetic protection, yet like the man on the bridge offers to help without taking responsibility for the other's well-being. The good and caring pastor may well be the one who risks appearing callous when refusing to deviate from a course of action when others see that course as too hard and difficult. The good and caring pastor might be the one who is clear about her boundaries and refuses to let others trespass those boundaries out of a deep sense of self-respect. The good and caring pastor may well be the one who risks appearing selfish by ensuring that her own spiritual, physical, and emotional needs are met so that she can attend to those she leads and for whom she cares!

Yes, a theology of the cross turns the tables and completely redefines our perceptions of what it means to be good. And just as importantly the theology of the cross turns the tables on our perception on where our power for ministry is located! In this regard, we need to be very clear that a theology of the cross does not do away with power as many tend to think. However, it does see power in a strange, paradoxical, and hidden way. This paradoxical view of power is critically important to pastoral leaders and caregivers, because the work of pastoral care and leadership is always about helping people contend with powers that are attempting to wrest their life away regardless of the form those powers may take. It is about helping people leave what is old for what is new, and that help cannot be offered without the pastoral leader and caregiver having a sense of where her own power is located. Yet as we have seen, under the cross this power is not like power in the world. It is strangely and paradoxically hidden in weakness and humanness. It is not a power that one creates for one's self, nor is it manifested in ways that are comprehended by the world. Yet it is power nonetheless, and it is a power that can be trusted to engage the destructive powers that seek to take life away from those who are entrusted to our care.

Implications for Pastoral Care and Leadership

The point of this chapter is that when pastors find themselves in the "condition of stuck" they are often caught in the tension between expectation and experience. They are working out of the expectation that to be a good pastor they must be unconditionally nice and loving, and that such niceness and unconditional love will win the day. Yet their experience is that these efforts are ineffective, and the chronic conditions they are trying to change continue to persist. However, the chronic condition many of us in ministry fail to recognize or do anything about is our own, namely the condition of masking our humanness behind a false piety that says we must be nice and loving in order to be a good person and a caring pastor. By humanness, I am referring to emotions and attitudes such as anger, resentment, sorrow, disappointment, grief, disillusionment, and the list could go on. Somewhere along the way, we learned that to have these sorts of feelings—much less give them any kind of outward expression—was antithetical to being good. Moreover, many of us grew up in environments where the expression of these emotions was in fact abusive and dangerous. Is it any wonder that we came to be afraid of them and have worked hard to repress them?

For most of us in ministry, the identity of pastor and minister has been a convenient way to keep this side of our humanness hidden and at bay. By its very nature, the office and role of pastor and minister gives us masks to wear. In some traditions we are given liturgical vestments and garments that enshrine us with a certain holiness. We are given the privilege and responsibility of the pulpit from which we are to bring a word from the Lord, which in and of itself enshrines us with holiness and power. We are generally given a certain respect in the community, invited to be a religious presence at public gatherings when asked to deliver invocations. Do not misunderstand, these are all vitally important and necessary roles for pastors and ministers. These are the sorts of things our office of pastoral care and leadership calls us to do. At the same time, however, their danger is that they often turn into a theology of glory because they become masks that hide the truth of who we really are. They turn us into "spiritual beings" who don't have anger, who don't feel despair, who don't grieve, who are always strong, and who seemingly have no weaknesses. The point of this chapter is that the more we live in pretense and illusion about our human condition, the less effective we are in helping others change their lives. From the point of view of a theology of the cross and in a paradoxical way, the very humanness we work so hard to hide and avoid may well be our most ardent gift for ministry. More to the point, the very humanness from which we are trying to run might well be the source of our power to engage the powers that be.

Throughout my practice, the most difficult struggle I have observed pastors have with their own humanness is with their anger. In our conventional way of thinking about caregiving and pastoral leadership, anger has no place. We work hard to keep it repressed and at bay. Yet after some twenty years of listening to countless call stories, I am convinced that anger is what brought us to ministry. I don't mean raging anger that is abusively out of control. The anger that brought us to ministry is the anger that tells us we don't like the way things are and we want to do something to change it. We don't like the way people treat each other; we don't like the injustices in the world; we don't like seeing people marginalized and living on the streets. The truth is we are angry about these things whether we acknowledge that anger or not. Our anger, not unlike many of the prophets, is what motivates us to cry out and help people see what is wrong. In a strange and paradoxical way, our anger is at the heart of our care! Anger, then is far from being something that is bad and demonic as many believe. It is actually a sign that tells us we care deeply about somebody or something!

Yet, from the very beginning of our pastoral formation, we work hard to keep anger hidden and tucked away. Good and caring pastors don't get angry. Good and caring pastors do not reveal that dark side of themselves. Good and caring pastors are to portray a gentle niceness to which others will positively respond. Where would prophets like Jeremiah be if they had had to work as hard at keeping their anger—either at God or at those for whom they cared—hidden and tucked away as we do? And why is it that we work so hard to keep anger hidden in our work of care? Why is it that we cannot see it as an invaluable part of our care for others?

As a way of illustrating what I'm advocating and how anger might be more a part of our care than we are want to believe, I'd like to revisit three vignettes—the story of Jan, the story of the pastor who escaped to the foxhole, and the story of the pastor who thought boundaries were bad—to illustrate how the use of anger might have changed the care and leadership they offered.

Jan, you will recall, was the CPE student who was trying to help a friend through the use of unconditional acceptance, yet in the process found herself angry at the way she was being manipulated and used. Moreover, she found herself stuck by her own understanding of what it means to be a good pastor, and it was this very understanding that drove her to deny how angry she was. Had she been able to access her anger earlier on in her attempts to help, she might have stated to her friend that she was deeply concerned about the way her friend was destroying her life, but that she was even more concerned about her unwillingness to take responsibility for herself. After stating her concern, she might have established clearer boundaries by indicating what she was willing to do and not do. So, for instance, she might have said, "I am more than happy to help you find a treatment center that will help you with your addiction problem. I will even drive you there and help you get admitted. I will assist you in finding the financial resources necessary to pay for this treatment. While you are in treatment, I will stand by you to offer whatever encouragement and support is needed. However, if you are unwilling to take any of these steps for yourself, I will not allow you to continue to call me and ask me to solve your problems. I cannot carry a burden that you are unwilling to carry for yourself."

Based on what we have been saying in this chapter, Jan could have used her anger to establish boundaries about what she was willing to do and what she was not willing to do. More importantly, by establishing these boundaries, her anger could have been used to help her turn responsibility back to her friend. Note that the use of anger does not mean that Jan has to explosively pour out her anger towards her friend, by no means. It simply means that she could have used her anger as a signal that she was stuck and that she need to reposition herself so that she would not be taking more responsibility for her friend's health and recovery than the friend was willing to assume for herself. Anger was actually Jan's best ally, but because it is something that she could not fathom as part and parcel of what it means to offer good pastoral care, it went unused, and as Jan came to realize, her pastoral care was not as effective as it could have been.

Like Jan, the pastor who retreated to the foxhole could not fathom anger as being part of his pastoral care and leadership. Yet it was clear he was quite angry at his detractors for their behavior and the way they were reacting to the changes he was initiating. In the language of systems theory, the pastor was reacting to the behavior of his detractors, and his reactivity was in the form of under functioning, that is, passively retreating to the foxhole. Bear in mind, that in systems theory language, the idea of self-definition does not mean having things go your way or that you will change others. It does mean, however, keeping yourself standing up and staying true to your directions in the face of criticism and outright sabotage. Thus, one of the ways his anger could have served him was to help him look deeper at the underlying values and core beliefs that were driving the changes he was initiating. By articulating these values and beliefs along with the vision they had engendered, the focus is taken off of the changes themselves, and it invites a more substantive conversation around how the congregation will be in mission. To be quite clear, if the pastor were to have used his anger in this way, the conflict would not have gone away.

In fact it would probably have worsened. However, the important thing is that the pastor's anger enables him to stand up to the powers that be with a more clearly defined position about what he is trying to do and why. This is, in fact, what the pastor did. His anger empowered him to leave the foxhole and to take a well-differentiated stand. As he began to articulate his vision with more clarity and by sending a clear signal that he was not going to retreat, the reactivity of his detractors diminished.

As with Jan and the pastor in the foxhole, the pastor who thought boundaries were bad could not fathom anger as part of her pastoral identity. Yet in the illustration given, she was clearly angry at the way members of the work group were sabotaging her leadership and the work that had been assigned to them. Had the pastor recognized her anger and utilized it, she might have recognized that her anger was sending her a clear signal that the group's sabotage was violating her own boundaries and not respecting its own process. With this in mind, she might have intervened, indicating her expectations of the group's behavior and that conversations and decisions made outside of the group's process were not appropriate. As in the previous illustrations, this change in position on the part of the pastor would not necessarily have removed the conflicts or issues that were driving the group's reactive behavior. However, it would have challenged the group to rise to a different level of functioning.

In all three of these illustrations, the use of anger would have changed the nature of the care and leadership that was offered. Some might have difficulty identifying it as pastoral. Yet as we have been saying throughout this discussion, it would be a care and leadership that challenges the recipient to rise to the occasion and move from what is old to what is new.

But why do we have such difficulty recognizing our anger and affirming it as a gift for ministry, care, and leadership? I suggest that the answer to that question is different for all of us, and it is embedded in our own family stories. While each of us brings a unique story to our formation work, I submit that the one common theme that keeps us from acknowledging our anger as an important part of our care and our calling is shame. I also submit that shame is a power that has brought many more of us to ministry than we care to admit. As I will say throughout the next chapter, this in no way discounts or discredits our calls to ministry, nor does it in anyway mean that we are ill equipped for the work we are called to do. But it does mean that we need to become much more aware of the extent to which it operates in our life and work, and the extent to which it robs us of using our full persons and selves—including our anger—in the work of caring for others. To an exploration of this we turn in the next chapter.

Questions for Discussion and Reflection

1. When did you first feel a stirring or sense that you were being called into ministry? What did you do with this stirring? Who did you talk to? How did you go about discerning whether or not you were being called?

2. What did you feel you were being called to do? Try to be as candid, forthright, and concrete as you can.

3. What expectations did you have of yourself in ministry? What sort of pastor or caregiver did you imagine yourself to be? What expectations did you have about what ministry would be like? Did you imagine people liking you? How did you imagine people would respond to your ministry? Did you imagine people getting angry at you? Did you imagine yourself getting angry at the people to whom you minister? Did you ever imagine yourself situated in the middle of a church conflict?

4. How does your *experience of ministry* compare with your *expectations of ministry*? Is ministry what you thought it would be? Has ministry provided you with the satisfaction and rewards you expected?

5. What "powers that be" have you encountered in your ministry? As you prepared for and entered ministry, did you expect to encounter these powers?

6. Have there been occasions in your ministry where you have had to rethink you vocational calling? What were those occasions? What happened and what were the questions that you were asking? What was the outcome of this rethinking? Did your ministry change? If so, how?

Four

From Niceness to Power— Rising to the Occasion

Power in Pastoral Care

Throughout this discussion we have asserted that niceness, the constant and persistent focus on feelings, and working harder to help people feel good are not sufficient to effect change, especially when the individual or organizational system are in the grasp of the powers that be. Moreover, such posture is inconsistent with biblical stories in which the one being called must exude strength and fortitude to say what needs to be said and to stand firm against the powers that seek to undo life and community. At the same time, there is something in most of us that continues to perpetuate the myth that good and caring pastors are pastors who help others feel good. Even as we cognitively know we are not defined by how others feel, there is nevertheless something that keeps us holding on to the myth that if we can just make others feel good, we ourselves will be good. Thus we work harder and harder in the same old way only to find ourselves perpetuating the condition of stuck.

We have also asserted that the work and purpose of pastoral care is about helping people leave what is old and move into what is new. Such movement, just like the Exodus, does not come without adversity or conflict. The powers that be—external and internal—will always rear their heads and sabotage change in an effort to return to homeostatic balance. Thus, the transition from what is old into what is new always requires that the one making the transition must "rise to the occasion." Pastoral care and leadership, therefore, is always about helping people do precisely that: *rise to the occasion.* This rising up to meet the challenges that face us does not come automatically or passively. It does not happen without intentionality, and it especially does not happen without accessing one's internal strength, fortitude, and inner spiritual power. Thus, this chapter explicitly argues that if the caregiver and the recipient of care are to rise to the occasion to meet the challenges they face, the work of rising to meet challenge requires putting away niceness and the focus on feeling good in order to access and utilize this God-given strength. Rising up to resist the powers that be will not occur if we remain focused on feeling good.

In every pastoral care and leadership event where an individual or congregational system is being called on to rise to the occasion, a parallel process is at work. Just as the individual or congregation must rise up to meet the challenge, so also the caregiver and leader must rise up to provide the required care. Make no mistake: the forces of sabotage and resistance are equally powerful in both the one being called to change *and* the one who is helping to facilitate that change. Thus transitioning from niceness to power so as to rise to the occasion must happen in both the pastoral caregiver as well as the recipient of that care. Our premise is that without such transition on the part of the caregiver and leader, change is not likely to happen in the recipient of care. Instead, both will likely stay stuck in the chronic condition that presented the challenge in the first place.

From Whence Comes our Niceness

The transition from niceness to power requires that we gain more clarity about what drives our niceness in the first place. What is so deeply embedded in our pastoral identities, motivating us to function out of niceness, even when we know differently? Until we have clarity and awareness around this matter, we can make all the external changes we want, but our deep need to please others and make them feel good will remain the chronic condition out of which we function! With this in mind, we begin by asking the question: from whence comes our niceness?

As we noted in the last chapter, most of us come to ministry with the desire to be good pastors, and we bring expectations of how that goodness will be achieved. These expectations do not fall out of the sky nor do they come upon us through some sort of divine intervention. We learned how to attain goodness early on in life and we learned it through the emotional systems in which me moved and had our being. In short, we learned how to attain goodness in both the emotional systems of our families of origin and in our church families. As with my own life, it was in these systems that we learned the rewards of being nice, and it was in these systems that our making others feel good was affirmed. To use system language, we learned "fusion" early on. Without knowing what was happening to us, many of us grew up in systems with persons who had no sense of self, no ability to take responsibility for their own emotional selves or well-being. Rather they depended on others—those like us—to "make them happy." We learned early on how to be on guard for their emotional states, and we learned almost instinctively how to adapt our behavior to theirs so that we might avoid dangerous emotional outbursts if not outright violence. In and through all of this, we learned, even if we could not understand it, that we were somehow responsible for the emotional state of those around us. If they were upset or angry, then surely we were somehow responsible for their problem. Even if we were not the cause of their discontent, we learned somehow that we were responsible to make it better. We learned the simple formula: if those dependent on us for their emotional well-being are happy, then we are good; if they are unhappy, discontent, and disquieted, we must make it better. It does not take long to see that for many of us—if not most—our niceness is a behavior we learned early as a way of being emotionally responsible for and taking care of those around us. It should be no surprise to see how this chronic condition continues in our pastoral care and leadership.

But an even more toxic dynamic was brewing as we adapted to the dependent and dangerous emotional processes swirling around us. That dynamic was shame! In learning to be responsible for the emotional well-being of others, we also learned that something was fundamentally wrong with us if we could not make them better. The sense that "something is wrong with me" is precisely the shame we have carried into our work of caregiving and leading. If somehow I am unable to make others feel good, then there is something wrong with me and I am not measuring up! This shame of "not measuring up" is deeper than guilt. Guilt is what we feel when we know we have done something wrong. It does not necessarily affect our overall sense of worth and self-esteem. Guilt is repairable. We can make amends and change our behavior towards the one who has been wronged through our action. With such "metanoia," guilt diminishes and the conscience becomes clear. But shame is much, much deeper and it pervades our entire being in a way that guilt does not. If guilt is the feeling that tells us we have done wrong, shame tells us that *we are bad in the heart and core of our being.* Shame carries the clear and unmistakable message that because something is fundamentally wrong with our being we are *less than* other human beings. It is this sense of being *less than* that drives us to work so hard at being good. It is what drives us to work harder and harder at helping those we serve to feel good. For when they finally feel good, we are no longer *less than.*

To be sure, shame has many sources and affects human beings in varied ways; however, it is not within the scope of this discussion to go into a psychological examination of these causes and their resulting behavior. Our focus is on the dynamic of being responsible for the emotional well-being of others and the shame that results whenever we are unable to fulfill that expectation. More to the point, our concern is to understand the extent to which this particular shame dynamic is operative when pastoral caregivers and leaders find themselves in the condition of stuck.

Regardless of its source, but most notably in the dynamic noted above, the one thing that all shame has in common is its ability to rob human beings of their power to be fully human. More to the point, shame is what leaves us feeling that others have power over us and the power to define us. Shame is what tells us that we do not have the right or ability to speak or stand up when others are dictating our actions or have control over us. In systems theory, shame is what decreases our capacity for self-definition. When we grew up in family, organizational, or community systems in which we had to contend with those kinds powers on a regular basis, we learned that survival depended on adapting or even cowering to them. For many of us, taking a defined position in opposition to those powers was risky; adaptivity was safer. If it is the case that many of us have come to ministry in an effort to find salvation from our shame—and I do believe this to be the case!—then it should be no surprise to us that when we come up against the powers that be in our ministry, whether those powers are in individuals or in our congregational organizations, we find it extremely difficult to take a stand. How many of us in conflicted situations find ourselves feeling helpless and powerless, as though the powers we are up against are stronger than we are? It is precisely in these moments—whether in our care of individuals or in our leadership of organizations—that we fall into the condition of stuck. It is in these moments that we find ourselves crying out, "I don't know what else to do." The point is this: when we come to this moment of stuck, when all else fails and we are crying out in exasperation that we have run out of resources, there is a very good chance that the source of our stuckness is not the absence of power, but rather the fact that our shame has reared its head, playing the same tricks it has played throughout all of our life. Our stuckness is the same stuckness we experienced when we came up against the powers that be in our family systems, when we found ourselves powerless to speak or stand up in the face of verbal, psychological, or even physical abuse. It is the same stuckness we knew when, despite our best efforts, we could not make others feel good. It is the same stuckness we felt when deep inside we wanted to cry out and say, "stop looking to me to make your life better; take responsibility for yourself!" but somehow could not because we knew what the consequences would be. When we come to these moments of stuck, it is not due to the absence of technique, but rather because shame has robbed us of the power to stand and speak!

Justified by Grace through Faith: Imbued with Power

What then is the antidote to this virus and malignancy that has so deeply and pervasively affected us? I have argued that the answer is not to be found in a technique or some faddish self-help formula. In the first chapter, we noted that when we arrive at moments of stuck, the clue to getting unstuck has to do with making an internal shift in how we think of ourselves and our pastoral vocation, not in learning a new technique. As we come face to face with the shame that robs us of the ability to lead and care out of our authentic selves, the clue is not learning a new how-to-do-battle-with-your-internal-demons technique, but rather in making an important internal shift in our thinking and attitude towards ourselves and our whole being. This internal shift does not happen automatically, nor is it something we can stir up within ourselves or by our own volition. No! It is a shift informed and shaped by an external Word, spoken to and about us by God, a Word that comes at us every day, a Word that unequivocally declares that we are created anew in the likeness and image of God to live within the power that God gave us! It is a Word that liberates us from the power of shame to be the authentic persons, caregivers, and leaders we were created to be in the first place. This is what Luther meant with his all too famous—and often misunderstood—formula, justification by grace through faith. To be justified is to be liberated from the grasp of shame's power! Thus the internal shift that is required to stand up to the power of shame does not come from our own ability to redefine ourselves. Rather it comes from believing and trusting what has already been created, redeemed, and renewed in us! It comes from believing, deep within our bones, that shame does not have the power we have given it. It comes from believing and trusting what has already been spoken and declared: you are no longer *less than*. Or, as Elias Chacour might say using his interpretation of the Beatitudes, "Rise up you who have been debilitated by shame! Rise up, you who have known nothing but *less than*." Indeed, to truly believe and trust we are justified by grace leads us to a radical and daring shift in our ability to care and lead.

However, in our American culture, salvation and justification by grace are not always understood in a way that is connected to power. More to the point, the way justification is preached from many pulpits tends to lead us in the direction of psychology and feelings: justification by grace means I can feel good about myself in spite of everything without any fundamental change in my relationships with others, particularly when it comes to thinking about my sense of personal power and how I use that power. In this regard, justification by grace is used as a quick fix to my psychological ache, but it does not require me to make the sort of internal shifts that will lead to my taking a new position in my family of origin or the organizational systems I lead.

As with interpretations of John 3:16, our understanding of justification by grace is that "God accepts me for who I am. God loves me in spite of myself." While God's unconditional regard for the human creature is clear, these kinds of interpretations of justification neither require nor lead to any change on the part of the believer. As a matter of fact, they perpetuate and sustain chronic conditions of stuckness. For pastoral caregivers and leaders, even though an immediate relief from feelings of shame and guilt might result from these messages, shame remains the dominant power that defines life and niceness remains the position from which care and leadership are offered. Unless the words of "forgiveness," "justification," and "new life" are given space to create a new way of thinking about one's self, sparking a new sense of power over that which has robbed one of life, unless they are allowed to speak the good news, "Rise up!" they will be no more than words that relieve our psychological ache, and they will not lead the caregiver or leader from what is old into what is new. If leaders are unable to appropriate these words of new life and power for themselves, they will remain unable to lead others into the same, remaining in the chronic condition of stuck.

By now, the reader may wonder if I am proposing a way of thinking about pastoral care that completely does away with the notion of empathic comfort. Does the suggestion that the caregiver must transition from niceness to power mean that there is no room for sensitivity to feelings? Not at all. Effective pastoral care must always begin with an empathic ear that seeks to hear and understand the life circumstances and emotions of the one to whom care is being extended. After all, the entire Exodus story begins with God hearing the cries of the enslaved, and knowing their plight deep within God's own being. But it is precisely in this story that we see the intrinsic connection between empathic hearing and power: God's empathic hearing stirs God's power. It is what leads to the Exodus intervention by which the people are led from what is old into what is new. Indeed, pastoral care and leadership can never be devoid of empathic listening, for it is only in empathic listening that the caregiver and leader can understand the circumstance of the one receiving care. It is only in empathic listening that the caregiver and leader can understand the transition through which the recipient of care must go. At the same time, however, empathic listening without power eventually leads to nothing more than sympathetic protection. Conversely, power without empathic listening leads to power misuse and abuse.

Pastoral caregivers and leaders tend to approach the subject of power with aversion, ambivalence, if not outright resistance. No wonder that this is so. Power as we know and observe it exercised in our culture is always associated with gaining the upper hand over an adversary or opponent, often with no concern for truth, character, or integrity. As is evidenced in so many of our political processes—government and church alike—the exercise of power is what takes place in attempts to dominate community life and force it into the acceptance of a certain ideology or way of thinking. Power is what is used to dominate others, and in its extreme abuses, power is used to keep others in subordination through coercive, manipulative, and violent means. In church life, stories abound of pastoral caregivers and leaders who in the name of self-differentiated leadership have exercised power in manipulative and coercive ways to get their own way, or worse yet, have exercised the power of the pulpit to shame their adversaries and opponents. With these sorts of images and stories, we are correct to be cautious and even suspicious about a conversation that suggests effective pastoral care and leadership requires persons to transition from niceness to power.

At the same time, power is not evil. The fact that persons inappropriately misuse and abuse power in their care and leadership does not mean that power is inherently bad. As with anger and other emotional dynamics viewed negatively and anathematic to good pastoral care and leadership, our task is to understand more clearly how power is a gift and how we might be its good stewards instead of its abusers. An underlying assumption of this discussion is that power is a major theme throughout the entire biblical narrative. The Exodus event does not happen without God exercising God's power to engage the Pharaoh. Time and time again, those whom God calls into service, regardless of the service, are called upon to exercise power to do what they have been called to do. It cannot be avoided. Persons can use the gift for the purposes it was intended, or they can use it to serve their own ends, which often leads to the abuses to which we have referred. Our task is to gain clarity about this power, increase our awareness of its dangers, yet work towards an integration of self that will enable one's self and others to rise to the occasion so as to move from what is old into what is new.

Four Case Studies

The following are four case studies that illustrate caregivers and leaders who made an intentional shift from niceness to power in order to free themselves and the persons for whom they were caring from the condition of stuck. Two of these cases are actual pastoral care events that took place with persons as they were confronted with serious illness, the impending death of a loved one, and significant life change. The third is an illustration taken from the medical profession in which an emergency room doctor is confronted with the problem of treating persons suffering from chronic pain with addicting narcotic pain medication. The fourth vignette is about a significant transition in the life of a congregation in which the reactive behavior of one of its so-called influential members is sabotaging its movement towards more effective missional outreach. In each of these incidents, the caregiver or leader is required to shift from niceness to power in order to help free the emotional system from its condition of stuck.

John

This is the case of John, a CPE student who was the chaplain in the cardiac intensive care unit of a children's hospital. As difficult as the situation is, it is common: a mother is faced with the terrible reality that everything to save her child has been done and continued life support is really a futile effort. The mother in this instance was a single parent, and John was the chaplain who had been visiting her and providing pastoral support from the time of her child's admission. John typically offered pastoral care out of his niceness. He was not a large man, yet strong in appearance, having played college basketball and baseball. When on the basketball court, he was competitive and challenging, using his strength in whatever way he could to block his opponent or make his way to the basket. When offering pastoral care, he was gentle, soft, and nice, never challenging or ever saying anything that would disrupt parents' or patients' homeostatic balance. In this particular case, the medical staff was keenly aware of the limits with which everyone was now challenged: nothing could any longer be done for the child. As is typical of many medical teams who give their all to revive and save life, they know when it is time to quit and make a decision. They would grow impatient if that decision was prolonged. Such were the dynamics in this event. Their attempts to tell the mother it was time to let go were met with understandable resistance and denial. She refused to let go and implored them to keep working. Interestingly, John was nowhere to be found in this conversation. He continued to visit and offer a palliative comfort that focused on her feelings. He acknowledged how terrible and awful this was, prayed for her comfort, and offered her consolation. Parallel to the mother's resistance to face the realities and grief in front of her, John resisted engaging these same realities as well. The system was stuck: the mother could not get off center to make the decision that needed to be made so everyone, including her child, could get on with life; the chaplain was stuck, refusing to utter the words, "It's time to let your child go"; and as a result, the staff was stuck in their anger towards the mother because she would not make a decision.

When confronted by his supervisor and peers about why he was so reluctant to confront the mother with the truth of the situation, John was challenged to examine the extent to which his personal and pastoral identity relied on his niceness. For John, good pastors don't make people hurt. To challenge the mother's denial and confront her with the truth of what was in front of her was beyond his concept of what it means to be a good pastor.

Knowing John's history as an athlete, his supervisor wondered if there was a way for John to employ the same inner power he used when he was playing basketball. This was a radical idea for John. The employment of power in his pastoral care was not something that had ever entered his thought process. To his credit, John took the challenge to heart. He went to visit the mother, only this time it was to offer something different. As he describes the event, he got on his knees and looked straight into her eyes and said, "Mary, it is now time to let your child go; for all purposes he is dead and we cannot save him." The truth was in front of her in a new and different way, and because of the way John now positioned himself with the mother, she could not retreat into denial or blind optimism. Not long after this conversation, life support was withdrawn and the child died.

I do not want to suggest that this event was as clean as it may sound. I suspect that the outpouring of grief as the decision was made was anything but nice and pretty. And that's precisely our point: when pastoral caregivers opt to provide a support that tries to keep persons from moving into the chaotic realities that are in front of them—as John was doing—stuckness will prevail. What happened in this scenario is that John made a crucial internal shift in his whole understanding of what it means to be a good chaplain, and in making that shift he helped facilitate the mother's movement from what is old into what is new, painful, and difficult as it was. When John transitioned from niceness into power, he facilitated a change in the whole system. To be sure, his exercise of power was not of the competitive sort that we would see on the basketball court. But it was power nonetheless! It was a power to stand up to the power of denial and illusion, a power to speak truth and say what had to be said. It was a power that enabled him to stand with the mother in a new and different way.

Beth

This is the case of Beth, whose husband was hospitalized for a debilitating stroke. She, too, was faced with a common scenario, namely the decision to transfer her husband to a nursing care facility against his wishes. The narrative presented here is a reconstruction of the conversation between Beth and one of the hospital chaplains. It should be noted that the chaplain and Beth had prior history with each other, so the conversation was able to move beyond the surface rather quickly. Seeing Beth in the hospital's coffee shop, the chaplain sat down and asked how she was doing. It did not take long for her to tell her story. Concern and anxiety were on her face. The stroke had left her husband debilitated enough that she knew it would be difficult at best to care for him at home. She herself suffered from a heart condition, and meeting the demands of his health care would bring increased risk to her own health. Her daughter who was close to giving birth was part of this conversation and asserted what seemed to be an obvious fact: the patient was not going to be able to come home. Beth, though, was not yet ready to accept this reality, although she seemed to know cognitively it was the decision that had to be made. She had been previously and was then the recipient of her husband's increased and intense demands to take him home. One can imagine the bind she felt, realizing her own limitation, yet at the same time wanting to be a "good wife" who was able to relieve her husband's anxiety. After listening for a while, the chaplain asked the wife, "How do you see all of this playing itself out? If this were a book, what's the next chapter?" She was taken back a bit by the question and said, "I never thought about it that way." She pondered, and then said, "I see him having to go to some sort of facility. There's no way I can handle him at home." The question invited her to look at and name the circumstance and occasion of change to which she needed to rise up. This in and of itself did not get her unstuck. She remained ambivalent: "I know that's what has to be done, but I just am not sure I can do that." The chaplain invited further exploration. He said, "I wonder what you imagine will happen if you place him in a facility." It did not take long for her to respond: "He will be upset, and I'm not sure I can live with that." The chaplain continued, "It sounds as if you won't be a good wife if you cannot make this all better for him, as if you will have failed." With tears in her eyes, she acknowledged this to be the case. In this brief exchange she named the existential reality keeping her stuck: her goodness as a wife was contingent upon her ability to make her husband "feel good." There was no way out of this bind if this was the lens through which she was to frame her circumstance.

From a systems perspective, the spouse is viewing this entire circumstance from what has been the homeostatic balance of their emotional system: her position is to assume responsibility for his emotional well-being. Her job—vocation if you will—was to help him feel good. As with most persons who find themselves in these circumstances, she had not had the opportunity to think critically about the position she assumed and how that position might actually perpetuate the chronic condition of emotional dependency rather than facilitate change.

Transitions from what is old into what is new can be seen at different levels in this scenario and they are all interlocking and interdependent. The most obvious transition is the husband's living situation. The new into which he and they needed to move was a new living arrangement that would attend to his nursing-care needs. But in order for this movement to occur, other transitions were also required. The spouse, for example, needed to reframe her sense of worth and goodness so as to rise to the occasion to place her husband in a facility against his strident and demanding objections. She needed to make an internal shift in her sense of self so that she would not be sabotaged by the belief that she was a bad person and wife if she could not make her husband happy. She was faced with the challenge of transitioning from her nice-ness to a new sense of power for herself that would enable her to do what had to be done. A third transition was the most difficult, and it likewise required a shift and move-ment towards a completely new perspective for the entire family, namely that the husband—sick though he was—had the responsibility to rise up to the occasion of the challenges in front of him. This was not something they had even considered, for like so many of us they were operating with the prevailing belief that because he was ill, he was relieved of being responsible for his emotional self. Like in the story about the bridge, Beth's husband continued to throw her the rope expecting she would save him without any effort on his part. And like the man on the bridge who kept holding on, the wife could not let go so long as she was unwilling or unable to let her husband be responsible for himself.[1]

From the chaplains' perspective, the key to this fam-ily's ability to transition from what was old into what was new was with Beth. In order to rise to the challenge of transitioning her husband to a nursing care facility, she needed to make the internal shifts noted above, however slight those shifts might have been. Rightly, the chaplain invited her into further conversation around the issue of her limits, wondering what it was like for her that she could not make any of this better and that she was un-able to take care of him at home. She responded by saying

1. Friedman, *Friedman's Fables*, 9ff.

how horrible it was, how guilty she felt, but then she also revealed she was feeling angry at him for placing these demands on her when she was faced with her own health issues and limits. These are dangerous thoughts for someone when his or her spouse is ill. We aren't supposed to get angry at people who are sick and can't take care of themselves. This powerful and operative belief contributes to maintaining the homeostatic condition of stuck, and it was doing so in this situation. At this point, the chaplain shifted his focus from feelings to thinking—a very significant shift. He affirms her anger, but then offers another lens through which to look at the situation. He pointed out that if she did take him home and try to take care of him she was risking her own death, at which point he would end up in a nursing home anyway. To take him home, although it might relieve immediate anxieties, would only worsen an already bad situation. Paradoxically, the attempt to be a good person and wife by relieving his anxiety and making him happy would actually contribute to everyone's demise. To her credit, Beth listened to what the chaplain offered her, and began to make the internal shift from feeling to thinking within herself. This does not mean she disregarded what she was feeling! By no means, but by shifting from feelings to thinking, she took away the power of guilt and shame that she unwittingly had allowed to define her. Once this shift occurred, she made the decision to transfer her husband to a nursing care facility where he died not long after.

Dr. J

Our third case takes a brief diversion from pastoral care to the practice of medicine. The dynamics of niceness and power are the same, however. Dr. J is a doctor in an urban hospital who has recognized the growing dilemma of persons who come to the emergency room to get addicting narcotic painkillers under the guise of treatment for chronic pain. More to the point, he came to realize he was complicit in the problem as he continued to give patients what they were asking for rather than intervene or refuse their requests. As Dr. J described his predicament, he was stuck. He was stuck between his abiding vocational desire to relieve people of their suffering and the fact that to give these particular patients the immediate relief they were seeking was to contribute to their addiction and ill-health. As he went on to say, "A job that once gave me enormous satisfaction was now sapping my energy. I didn't want to go to work anymore."

One of the complicating factors in this scenario is the matter of patient satisfaction. As in most hospitals, the entire medical staff is measured in large part by whether or not patients are satisfied with the care they receive. Even more pressure is put on staff by the fact that patient satisfaction plays a large part in government reimbursement programs. The bottom line is that doctors and nurses do not want patients to go away dissatisfied or unhappy. Given what is at stake, we can appreciate the condition of stuck in which Dr. J found himself. Using the language of our discussion, Dr. J's approach to and acquiescence of patients' demands was his niceness in action. He didn't want to offend anyone or get into conflicts, and he wanted patients to be happy and satisfied for the sake of good patient satisfaction scores. Not unlike pastors, Dr. J found himself in the predicament of basing his goodness as a doctor on making patients happy rather than on practicing good and sound medicine. He began to realize that the cost of such "goodness" was his own integrity and authenticity as a doctor. He noted, for example, that in these situations he often hurried in and out of the room without taking time to inquire about the patient's life circumstance and situation. And just as importantly he recognized that he had often dispensed prescriptions against his better medical judgment. In effect, he was not practicing the kind of medicine he felt called to practice.

Rather than sit back and let the power of addicted patients have their way and continue to deplete his energy, Dr. J began to think of a different approach. He initiated a program in the hospital's emergency room that created various markers by which persons suspected of narcotic abuse could be identified. Some of these markers included the frequency of emergency room visits within a particular time frame and the nature of their pain request. Several patients, for example, were adamant about the type of drug they wanted, suggesting a well-developed addiction to that particular drug. More importantly, Dr. J recognized that if he was to effect a change that would decrease the amount of addicting drugs being given by the emergency room, he would need to change his personal approach to these patients. So in addition to creating a departmental program, Dr. J shifted his position in relationship to narcotic-seeking patients. Instead of hurrying in and out of a room, he began to take time to talk with them and inquire about their life. In many cases he refused to comply with the patient's request, instead encouraging them to seek a different kind of help.

We can recognize Dr. J's transition from niceness to power and the effect that transition has on the department and on the patients that are served. Dr. J has no illusions about the effect of these changes on individual patients. Some patients simply leave when they realize they will not get what they want. Others, he realizes, will simply find another emergency room that will cater to their desires. Nevertheless, the changes he has initiated, both within the department and in his own practice, are significant and have had made a difference. The emergency room's pharmacy, for example, has seen a remarkable decrease in the number of narcotic pain medications it has dispensed since the program began. Perhaps the most important change, however, is in Dr. J himself. He is no longer stuck, and those with whom he works also feel a sense of power when they encounter drug- and narcotic-addicted patients.

Pastor B

Our fourth and final case is a pastor who within the first few months of arriving at his church encountered systemic resistance and sabotage from certain members. Their reactive and destructive behavior was not only aimed at the pastor but at other leaders and members of the congregation's governing board, some of it outright abusive. This particular congregation had a long history of power conflicts, especially after their considerably long-tenured and well-loved pastor retired. He himself had exercised a great deal of power and control over the congregation's life and work, and the congregation had settled into a homeostatic comfort with that arrangement. Pastor B was the third pastor to arrive after the long-tenured pastor had retired. The previous two pastors exercised completely different styles of leadership, the first being somewhat autocratic, the second being more passive and "pastoral," pastoral here referring to the sort who tries to affect change by being nice.

This vignette actually begins before Pastor B's arrival. One of the very wealthy and influential members of the congregation had lobbied to become part of the search committee that would eventually call Pastor B; however, he was not appointed by the governing board to the committee, much to his disappointment and anger. As he had done with Pastor B's predecessor, this particular person wanted to exercise power, influence, and control over the pastoral office. He had been somewhat successful with the previous pastor, due mostly to the pastor's reluctance to challenge or confront him.

Not long after Pastor B's arrival, two of the members of the governing board who had been instrumental in calling Pastor B began to receive abusive and threatening phone calls from this member, and from the tone of the phone calls they recognized his inebriated state. The phone calls were not isolated events. The recipients of the call reported the situation to Pastor B, who immediately recognized that the member's behavior was a power that needed to be reckoned with, not because it was a power that was directed at him or standing in his way. It needed to be reckoned with because it was interfering in the life of the congregation, and just as importantly, it was a power that was attempting to sabotage the call and work of the congregation's elected leaders.

It should be noted that in his previous ministries Pastor B had training and experience in community organizing, so he came into this situation with an awareness and understanding of how the powers that be work in community life. Out of this background, he understood that power is either "over/under" or it is "power with." From his perspective, all relationships hold the potential for transformation, and community life is always about transformation—the transformation of individuals and the transformation of the community itself. Such transformation does not happen unless the gift of power is used and exercised the way it was intended. Pastor B immediately recognized that while the recalcitrant member's behavior could be attributed to a problem with alcohol, it was also a problem of power. In attempting to intimidate some of the congregation's elected leaders, the member was attempting to gain power over them, just as he had done with previous pastors.

In the past, this person's behavior had been tolerated and even excused on the basis of his problem with alcohol—not to mention he was the congregation's largest giver. Some had even intervened, although their intervention was more like the story of Jan in the first chapter: one who tried to suggest he get help, yet never directly challenged his irresponsibility for fear of sending a signal of rejection and shame. In contrast to the conventional wisdom he learned at seminary—that pastors should never make any drastic moves in their first year in a congregation—Pastor B opted for a direct and radical intervention. Recognizing that this person's behavior toward the leaders was an outright interference with their ability to exercise the duties they had been elected to perform, he chose to take the matter directly to the governing board and bring it into the open, however, not before having a conversation with the members' spouse, who was herself a member of the governing board.

Pastor B invited the spouse into his office for a meeting and in a matter-of-fact manner laid out the problem and what he intended to do. As one might expect, the spouse reacted quite vehemently, suggesting that what Pastor B was about to do was "un-Christian and uncaring." To his credit, Pastor B held his ground and responded with the biblical admonition that such matters should always be taken to the ruling elders of the church. Basically, he told her he was simply doing what the Scriptures admonished him to do. As one can imagine, the meeting between Pastor B and the spouse did not end with any good will.

Pastor B took the matter to the governing board and asked that it send a letter to this particular member admonishing him to cease and desist his abusive behavior towards Pastor B and members of the governing board. Interestingly, the action of the governing board did not create much reactivity within the congregation. The member and his spouse immediately left the congregation, and the congregation, its new pastor, and its governing board went on with its work.

In reflection, Pastor B noted that what he had learned about power and transformation through his work in community organizing clearly informed the position and approach he took in this scenario. But he also recognized another dynamic at work, one that is much deeper. Pastor

B notes that he comes from a highly dysfunctional family with a mother who suffered from severe mental illness. Within this emotional system, he continually lived in fear that he would somehow be found responsible for whatever outbreaks or disruptions might occur. As he noted, his default position has always been, "I will be wrong." We can appreciate how this power was at work as he anticipated bringing this entire matter out into the open. We can also appreciate the internal shift that he had to make so as not to be defined by the voice that always says, "You will be wrong."

Pastor B's intervention and approach to this situation does not resolve the predicament in the manner that most of us would hope. The member and his spouse angrily reacted to the confrontation by moving their membership to another congregation, and they remained in their homeostatic condition. Yet, because of Pastor B's intervention, the congregation was not stuck nor fused to the member's disruptive and destructive behavior as it had been in the past. More to the point, with such freedom its leadership was now able to move forward with more constructive and life-giving endeavors. We should not be so naive as to think that this congregation is free of conflict. It is not. Conflict and disagreement seem to be part of its nature. At the same time, and in large part due to the position that Pastor B takes, its attitude towards the conflict is different. Conflicts seem to be less explosive and life threatening to its work and mission. More to the point, the congregation and its pastor seem less vulnerable to the condition of stuck than in the past.

What Can We Learn from these Three Cases?

1. *In each case, an internal shift takes place before there is an external action.* At the heart of this internal shift is a reframing of what it means to be good. The extent to which that internal shift happens determines the ability of the caregiver or leader to stand amid the powers that be, regardless of where those powers are situated and how they operate.

In the first chapter of this discussion we noted that when pastors are feeling stuck, the cause of their stuckness is internal, not external, and thus the required shifts are also internal! These shifts have everything to do with becoming aware of the "powers that be" operating within one's self and where those powers come from. It is a bit analogous to Jesus and the demons. Jesus has power over the demons in so far as he is keenly aware of and recognizes them. He is able to converse with them and so doing takes away their power. Until one recognizes what these powers are within one's self, including one's own family of origin, and until one also recognizes that these powers and sources of shame do not have to shape one's identity, the internal shifts to which I am referring are not likely to happen. In each of these cases, that awareness occurs at varying levels. Before John could access his inner power, he had to gain clarity around why he had invested so much in his niceness and why he was afraid of the power that had served him in athletic competition. He had to reframe not only his conceptual understanding of what it meant to be a good chaplain, but at a deeper level he had to reground himself in such a way to *believe* that he would *be* a good chaplain if he were to risk leading someone into disquieting feelings. In the same way, Beth, even in her brief encounter with the chaplain, gained an awareness of the extent to which she had based her goodness on her ability to remove her husband's anxieties. She was good when he was feeling good. The power with which she had to contend was his anger, but even more powerful was the shame she felt for her inability to remove it. Once she was able to make even a slight shift in this belief, she was able to make the decision that had to be made. Likewise, Dr. J and Pastor B make significant shifts in their self-definition of what it will mean to be a good doctor or good pastor. Dr. J's interest shifts his investment from making people feel good to practicing good medicine that helps people find health. Pastor B is not interested in whether or not the member and his spouse are happy and feel good. His goodness is predicated on helping the church leaders do their job without being sabotaged and in helping the congregation out of its stuckness.

But the shift that takes place in each of these cases—and it is the shift that is required for all caregivers and leaders—is not simply a matter of changing our conceptual understanding of the basis of our goodness. It is a shift that must take place deep in our being because it is a shift in what we believe! Before John could actually confront the mother about her son's condition he had to make a shift not only in what he thought, but what he would believe and rely on for his sense of goodness, especially in the face of the mother's intense reactivity. Would he continue to believe he was responsible and therefore a bad chaplain if his words drove her into intense grief? The same is true for Beth. She had to make a shift not only in what she *thought* was the basis for being a good spouse, but in whether or not she would truly believe this and trust it in the face of her husband's demands and anger, all reactions that had heretofore elicited her shame. Dr. J must redefine that being a good doctor is not about helping people feel good if it means staying in their addictive state. Pastor B must retune the inner voice that always says he "will be wrong" when there is disruption in the system. Any person who faces the "powers that be," regardless of where he or she is situated, must make this critical internal shift. This is Walter Wink's point in his commentary on Jesus' teaching about turning the other cheek and giving one's shirt. The ability of the slave to stand up to the one beating him and turn the cheek so as to diminish the master's power begins not with an increase in external and physical strength. It begins with an internal shift that completely changes the slave's self-identity and sense of goodness. It begins with an internal shift in believing who or what will define him.[2]

What I hope the reader sees here is that the hardest work any of us have to do in situations where individuals, organizations, or systems are at risk of getting stuck is to deal with our internal voices of shame that inhibit us from rising to the occasion. If leaders or caregivers are unable to do this within themselves, then the individual or organization receiving their leadership and care are at risk of allowing "powers that be" within the system to sabotage the transition from what is old into what is new and things will stay stuck.[3] It is an axiom in systems

2. Wink, *The Powers that Be*, 98ff.

3. Here I am making a direct link between Wink and Friedman. What Wink refers to as "the powers that be" are what Friedman calls the "viruses and malignancies" of an organization or emotional system.

theory: when the caregiver and leader attends to his or her own anxiety and ensures that he or she is standing forth amid the anxieties and the chaos of the moment, those who are receiving his or her care and leadership are more likely to follow suit and will find the internal strength and fortitude to do the same.

2. *The shift in determining the basis for one's goodness leads to a shift in vocation.*

When I speak of a shift in vocation, I do not necessarily mean a change in one's overall sense of call and life direction. John's larger vocational calling does not change. Neither does Beth's, Dr. J's, or Pastor B's. There is nevertheless a radical shift, however insignificant it might seem, that changes how they will position themselves in relationship to the circumstances they are up against. It is this repositioning that I am suggesting is a shift in vocation. In each case, the caregiver or leader must make a conscious decision about what one will be about in relation to those to whom he or she is extending care and leadership. They must make a conscious decision about what his or her care and leadership will focus on and what it will not focus on.

What happened for each of these persons was a shift that did not allow shame to be in the driver's seat, even though it might have been a constant presence in and through everything. To be sure, in each of these cases all sorts of "powers that be" operated at varying levels; however, the most important powers to which each needed to pay attention and with which each needed to wrestle were the internal powers of shame. And herein lies the point of this whole discussion: to give shame its power is to succumb to a pastoral vocation that focuses on feelings and sees helping people feel good as its primary objective rather than helping them rise to the occasion to meet the challenges in front of them. The power to help people rise to the occasion to meet whatever challenges they face comes from the external Word of God, which gracefully declares our entire identity, being, and goodness as rooted and grounded in God's faithful creativity, not in our ability to provide quick fixes and alleviate the anxiety and dis-ease of others.

3. *While the caregiver/leader in each case has deep empathy for the circumstance of those receiving his or her care and leadership, it is only when the focus is shifted from feelings to calling forth a new reality—thereby facilitating the transition from what is old to what is new—that stuckness is avoided.*

At no time in each of these cases is the caregiver/leader unaware of or insensitive to the emotions and feelings of those receiving his or her care and leadership. John is acutely aware of what the mother is going through and will go through, and he would like to help her avoid those feelings if at all possible. Beth is acutely aware of her husband's agony and the distress his illness is causing him. Dr. J is quite aware that persons asking for addicting pain medications have something going on in their life from which they are seeking an escape. Pastor B was astutely aware of the member's problem with alcohol and how it might be affecting the spouse and their family life. At the same time, in each of these cases, it is only when the focus of the caregiver/leader shifts from those feelings to the work of calling forth a new reality that the emotional process avoids stuckness. And each of them in their own way does in fact call forth a new reality on the part of the one who is receiving their care. By telling the mother that it is now time to let her child go, John calls forth in her a new way of being in relationship to her child's impending death, namely to face the truth that her child will die. Beth calls forth in her husband a new reality to which he will have to adjust rather than have her acquiesce to his demands. Dr. J calls forth a new reality in his patients by refusing to comply with their requests for addictive narcotics, but instead offers them other alternatives for managing their pain and life. Pastor B clearly calls forth new behavior on the part of the abusive parishioner and his family as well as on the part of the governing board.

Suggesting that effective care and leadership focuses less on feelings and more on the process of transition does not in any way mean that feelings are avoided, shunned, or discounted altogether. As we have noted throughout this discussion, however, there is a point at which the one giving care and leadership must move beyond sympathetic protection to empathic action so as to call forth and facilitate the change with which the emotional system is faced. Such is the circumstance in each of these cases. Once John moved beyond his niceness and was able to speak truth to the mother about her child's condition, the whole process moved off center, became unstuck, and began the movement from old into new. If all he had to offer was sympathy for her condition, stuckness would have prevailed, and he would have remained a complicit and willing participant in her stuckness. Only when Beth gives up trying to placate her husband's anger is the emotional process able to move forward. Likewise, when Dr. J begins to pay less attention to patients' feelings and more on finding ways to help them get healthier, he is able to stand stronger in his vocational calling.

4. In each of these cases, care and leadership are part and parcel of the same activity. The extent to which they are integrated depends in large part on the authenticity of the caregiver/leader.

Critical to John's care for the mother was his leading her into a transition. He recognized that she, nor her child, nor even the medical staff, could have life until she was able to enter this transition. This was not a transition that she could enter under her own power. Her own "powers that be"—and we can probably and safely assume they had to do with voices that told her being a good mother meant keeping her child alive regardless of his condition—had her in bondage so she could not move forward. She needed someone to lead her, and John eventually steps up to the plate to provide that leadership. His leadership is not overbearing, but it is a confronting leadership nonetheless. He speaks a truth to her she must hear, and it is a truth that no longer protects her from the realities that have up to this point been avoided. But at no time is this leadership disconnected from his care. As a matter of fact, it is out of his intense care for the mother that he leads her into a truth she has long feared and denied. He confronts her with a reality she can no longer deny or avoid, and in this regard John's ministry is prophetic and priestly at the same time. It is once and at the same time leadership and caregiving. He is concerned for the mother's future, for the child's future, and for the staff's future. It is out of this concern that he speaks the prophetic and priestly word.

Interestingly, when John confronted the mother with the realities in front of her, he discovered that his pastoral care was more authentic, more consistent with his personal identity and theology, and hence more self defined. It was more authentic because he was engaging the mother out of genuine concern and even anger at her resistance to let go. This authenticity is exactly what Friedman is talking about in his concept of self-differentiation.[4] Self-differentiation is not about getting one's own way. It is about having clarity and presence with one's own position, thinking, vision, and emotionality. As John began to understand that he had genuine concerns for this mother's well-being, and as he began to realize she could not get from what was old to what was new without some painful work, his entire pastoral presence changed. The more authentic and self-defined he became the more he engaged the mother with leadership and care. Beth's case is also similar. Once she became aware of her own dynamics and the extent to which she was taking responsibility for something she could not fix, she was able to engage the situation and her husband from a different position, one through which her care was expressed in leading her family into a new living situation! She was able to move into this leadership position only as she became more authentic with herself as well as with her husband.

5. *In each case, the self-differentiation on the part of the caregiver or leader is not about winning, getting one's way, or having power over another. It is simply about defining one's self and acting out of that self-differentiation so as not*

4. See Friedman, *Failure of Nerve*, 158ff.

to have one's integrity robbed by the destructive behavior of others.

Beth is not trying to win a battle with her husband to see who is right or wrong. She knows, however, that if she adapts to his wishes, neither of them will have much chance at life. Her health will be jeopardized, which in turn will prevent him from getting the care he needs. Her decision had a bigger picture than whether or not she is right or wrong.

Dr. J noted that the more he found himself adapting to the desires and wishes of addicted patients seeking prescription drugs, the less energy he had for a profession that had heretofore given him a deep and abiding passion. What he was describing was that his integrity was being robbed and he had to find a way to reclaim it. More to the point, he found himself in a position in which he was not practicing the kind of medicine he thought was good. He was violating his own conscience and standards. His reclamation is not about winning the battle with addicted patients. It is simply about defining what kind of doctor he will be or won't be. Yet in making this critical choice— regardless of whether addicted patients will change or not—he stands up and indicates that he will not participate in their illness, thereby reclaiming his vocational call and passion.

Likewise, Pastor B is not trying to win a battle with the member or gain the upper hand. He has a much bigger picture in mind as he intervenes, and that picture is about the long-term work and health of the congregation. It is not about who is right or who is wrong. It is about how the congregation will function and whether or not it will be able to be a congregation able to offer transformation to itself and the community around it. More to the point, Pastor B recognizes that by adapting to the behavior of the member, both he and the congregation's leaders will have sacrificed their integrity and the vocation to which they have been called.

Conclusion

This chapter is entitled, "From Niceness to Power—A New Way of Caring." In most caregiver's conventional way of thinking about pastoral care, niceness and caring usually go hand in hand, while caring and power are like vinegar and water: they don't mix. But the power I have been trying to illustrate in these cases is not a power manifested in coercion, control, or manipulation. It is not an over/under power that attempts to control the other. To use Walter Wink's image, it is a power that seeks to restore one's own integrity, dignity, and authenticity in the face of debilitating shame. Or as Elias Chacour would say, it is a power that empowers us to rise up. When we think of power in this way, then without question it must be coupled with caring. To offer care without this kind of power is to offer nothing more than palliative comfort, and when persons are faced with the sorts of challenges that come with grief, tragedy, loss, and major life disruption, palliative comfort in and of itself is not enough. Niceness must give way to power so that the care offered enables and empowers the recipient to rise to the occasion to move from what is old into what is new.

We began this discussion suggesting that when pastors get stuck and find themselves exasperated and not knowing how to get unstuck, it is a sure sign that the answer is to be found in rethinking one's pastoral call and vocation, not in finding a new technique. That is to say, it requires rethinking what we are to be about and how we will position ourselves in whatever circumstance is requiring our care and leadership. What I hope the reader will have heard in this conversation is that this rethinking involves a deeper consideration and reframing of what it means to offer care. Indeed, we are called to embody the care and compassion we see God extending to God's people throughout all of Scripture. We are called to offer care and leadership to individuals and communities that will help them rise with power to meet the everyday events and occurrences that threaten to rob them of life, integrity, and dignity. As pastoral caregivers and leaders we face these same threats! And as we have seen, the most powerful threat that we face is our own systemic shame. If we are to offer the kind of care and leadership that empowers others to withstand the "powers that be" in their own lives, then we must find and appropriate a way to withstand those same threats within ourselves. In this regard, we must remember that the good news of the resurrection means we are now defined by something other than our shame! This is not just an emotional or psychological phenomenon. We are a people and profession endowed with a power to care in a new way. When all else fails, remember that the power of resurrection is yours! When all else fails, live, care, and lead in that power!

Questions for Discussion and Reflection

1. If you have not done so, complete your family genogram. (Various resources, including those online, are available to help you develop and work with yours.) Reflecting on your family of origin and its emotional system, what was your position? Were you the peacekeeper, the oldest responsible child, the agitator, etc.? How did your position contribute to maintaining homeostatic balance? What position or positions did other family members assume? How did these positions serve the homeostatic balance?

2. How, within your family of origin's emotional system, did you become a good person? How was being a good person defined? Was being good the same for everyone in the system, or was being a good person different for different members? How was being a good person connected to your position in the system? What happened in the system if you took a more self-defined position or a position different from what the system expected of you?

3. Who in your family of origin shamed you or left you feeling less than? What is your awareness of these dynamics, and what is your awareness of how these dynamics affect your care and leadership? Who are the person or persons in your congregation who are able to shame you and leave you feeling less than? Is there any connection between how you function with them and how you functioned with similar persons in your family of origin?

4. In this chapter we have asserted that effective care and leadership require pastors to function from a position of power rather than niceness. What images of power do

you bring to your ministry practice? Where did these images come from? What is their impact on your ministry practice, your care, and your leadership? Do you embrace or avoid power? What theology informs your embrace or avoidance of power?

5. What would an effective use of power look like in your ministry practice? What shifts in position are required of you to function out of the power that you imagine? What enables or prevents you from making these shifts?

Afterword

Three after effects of reading this text will remain with me for a long time to come. The first is appreciation for Wayne Menking's capacity to demonstrate the art of self-definition in reflecting on Edwin Friedman's *The Failure of Nerve*. Menking offers a strong argument for the merits of Friedman's work, finding in it both an explanation and remedy for what he calls "the condition of stuck" that many pastoral leaders and congregations experience today. He enthusiastically and at times critically engages Friedman's ideas from a pastoral care perspective, especially in his discussion of empathy. Applauding the capacity for self-definition (a hallmark Friedman assertion about what it means to be a well-functioning human being), Menking also affirms the importance of being able to convey a genuine understanding of the convictions, values, and perspectives of those who think differently, and takes issue with Friedman's negative portrayal of empathy (arising from Friedman's observations about those who use the word "empathy" as a defense against assertive action). As Menking shows, empathy and self-definition do not need to be framed in opposition to each other, and what many people mean when they use the term "empathy" is much closer to sympathy. The capacity to convey understanding of the perspectives, thoughts, and feelings

129

of others, which Menking distinguishes from "protective sympathy," is one crucial aspect of the commitment to respectfully relate to others in ways that foster their agency and accountability. I have found few applications of the family systems theory of Murray Bowen (or the work of Friedman, one of Bowen theory's most ardent and well-known proponents) that not only enthusiastically affirm the theory but also engage it in a constructively critical way. This book demonstrates something of the appreciative *and* critical engagement that I look for in theological and pastoral applications of psychotherapeutic theory.

A second after effect is a deeper awareness and respect for the distinction Menking drives home throughout this text between *caring for* and *taking care of.* Speaking from the social locations he has served as pastor, administrative leader and teacher, and CPE supervisor, Menking observes that care as "niceness" too often trumps the kind of care that arises from deep respect for the agency and accountability of others as co-citizens of their families, congregations, and world. Friedman's work inspires him to review examples encountered in his ministry of supervision where the fear of speaking one's truth in caring ways (self-definition) reduces the practice of pastoral care to "niceness," and helpfully illustrates alternative approaches that help the pastoral caregiver move from the "condition of stuck" to more empowering ways of expressing deep care. Perhaps especially for those of us who have been deeply influenced by theological heritages that emphasize the primacy of God's grace (understanding that grace to be empowering in and of itself) and eschew "works righteousness," Menking's call to deeper theological reflection on the relationship between grace and responsibility and his contention that the interplay between certain cultural and theological ideas has indeed contributed to a widespread loss of nerve in pastoral leadership. He has already challenged me to observe more carefully my own interactions with others.

Finally, I gladly take to heart and will continue to reflect on Menking's ever-present effort to articulate a theology of pastoral care and pastoral leadership that witnesses to a conviction biblical scholar Walter Brueggemann voiced many years ago: "There are no personal issues that are not of a piece with the great public issues. To divide things up between the pastoral and the prophetic is to betray both."[1] Wayne Menking has worked to keep these aspects of the pastoral vocation integrated in this book, with the help of Friedman's theoretical work and illuminating connections with the work of New Testament scholar Walter Wink, and out of his own ministerial experience with those so deeply impacted by systemic injustice. This book challenges us all to do this work, and for that challenge I am profoundly grateful.

Kathleen D. Billman

Lutheran School of Theology at Chicago

1. Walter Brueggemann, *The Hopeful Imagination: Prophetic Voices in Exile* (Philadelphia: Fortress Press, 1986), 18.

Bibliography

Capital University. "Can Teaching Empathy Lead to Social Change?"
  Capital Magazine 29:2 (Summer 2011) 4–8.

Chacour, Elias. *Blood Brothers.* Grand Rapids: Chosen, 2003.

Clark, Arthur J. "Empathy and Sympathy: Therapeutic Distinctions
  in Counseling." *Journal of Mental Health Counseling* 32:2 (April
  2010) 95–97.

Friedman, Edwin H. *A Failure of Nerve.* Edited by Margaret M.
  Treadwell and Edward W. Beal. New York: Seabury, 2007.

———. *Friedman's Fables.* New York: Guilford, 1990.

———. *Generation to Generation: Family Process in Church and
  Synagogue.* New York: Guilford, 1985.

Hall, Douglas John. *The Cross in our Context: Jesus and the Suffering
  World.* Minneapolis: Fortress, 2003.

———. *Lighten Our Darkness: Towards an Indigenous Theology of the
  Cross.* Philadelphia: Westminster, 1976.

Luke, Timothy. "From Fundamentalism to Televangelism." *Telos* 58
  (Winter 1983–84) 204–10.

Luther, Martin. "Commentary on the Magnificat." Translated by A.
  T. W. Steinhauser. Vol. 21 of *Luther's Works.* Edited by Jaroslav
  Pelikan. St. Louis: Concordia, 1956.

———. "The Heidelberg Disputation." Translated and edited by
  Harold J. Grimm. Vol. 31 of *Luther's Works.* Edited by Helmut T.
  Lehman. Philadelphia: Muhlenberg, 1957.

Wink, Walter. *The Powers that Be: Theology for a New Millennium.*
  New York: Doubleday, 1999.